Carter House Cookbook

CARTER HOUSE

COOKBOOK

Mark & Christi Carter

TEN SPEED PRESS
Berkeley, California

1🟤
Ten Speed Press
Box 7123
Berkeley, California 94707

Cover design by Nancy Austin
Interior design by Sweet Forever
Cover photos by Patricia Brabant and John Swain

Library of Congress Cataloging-in-Publication Data

Carter, Mark, 1952–
  The Carter House cookbook from the Carter House/Hotel Carter/Mark Carter with Christi Carter.
    p. cm.
  Rev. ed. of: Carter House cookbook. Hotel Carter/by Denise and Michael Shumway, with Christi Carter and Mark Carter. ©1991.
  Includes index.
  ISBN 0-89815-773-0 (pbk.)
  1. Cookery, American--California style.   2. California, Northern--Social life and customs.   3. Carter House Inn (Eureka, Calif.)   4. Hotel Carter (Eureka, Calif.)   I. Carter, Christi, 1951–   II. Shumway, Denise, 1953–   Carter House cookbook, Hotel Carter.   III. Title.
TX715.2.C34C39   1995
641.5′09794′12--dc20   95-7447
                                                                                                   CIP
                                                                                                   REV.

Printed in Canada
1   2   3   4   5   6   7   8   9   10 — 99   98   97   96   95

For Joseph, Paul, Anne,

and Elenor

To Howard Tony
Happy Life Together!
Happy Cooking!
To a great friendship!

Mark and Christi

CONTENTS

Car trips are an American institution. Most of us have vivid childhood memories of being whisked down the road towards some unfamiliar destination, the scenery barely visible from our lowly vantage points. Dads were often the drivers. Most of us had a sibling giving us misery in the back seat. Moms served as mediators, relief drivers, and dispensers of placating goodies.

For many of us, these trips were the closest we came to high adventure. The idea of starting the morning at home and ending the day in some far away place was romantic, exciting, and stimulating. So much so that our moms and dads were willing to risk the certain choruses of "When are we going to get there? I have to go to the bathroom! He won't leave me alone!" to travel down the highways into the sunset.

Even in times of fuel economy and economic restraint, our annual venture down American highways and back roads is important enough that we will sacrifice in other areas of our lives to make it happen. These expeditions into the landscape keep us in touch with our heritage, renew our spirit of adventure, refresh our eye for beauty, and fulfill our need for change.

True travelers rarely take the main highways. The interstates are designed for convenience, not adventure. This is an understandable circumstance. Our parents, and perhaps grandparents, are full of stories of excursions that were a bit too challenging. Travel before the development of the interstate highway system involved long stretches of road with the availability of gas uncertain, the rest room facilities nonexistent, and the accessible food supply reduced to what you carried in paper bags in the trunk. In those days, the endless backdrop of rural scenery was a glut on the market. Most everyone came from small towns or farms. The idea that our soul needed such sights must have seemed ludicrous to many.

These days, however, more of us live in large cities than in the country. Our need to travel the less taken road has grown as our lives have become more autotomized, homogenized, synthesized. The wonderful old highways of this country are still there for us to use, but often they are neglected and ignored in these days of interstate travel. Some of these roads are better known than others; Highway 1, Route 66, The Blue Ridge Parkway, The Natchez Trace Highway. These roads are a part of our culture. Even those of us who have never ventured down these roads know of them from tales shared with us by romantic adventurers, an older family member, or television reruns.

These roads are like archeological sites, revealing to us in the scenery the layers of our cultural past. From the farmlands, where the people still earn their living through a harmony with the earth and where an occasional barn is painted with advertisements, to the villages that have seen better days, to the resilient small towns that have adapted yet maintained their integrity, to the urban sprawl that illustrates our dash for economic expansion, these roads remind us of the triumphs of our grandparents and the costs those triumphs demanded.

Along the less traveled roads, we find buildings with names like Ramblin' Rose Square Dance Hall, Twin Pines Motor Lodge, Sit a Spell Cafe, Chat 'N Chew Pancake House, and Klean and Kozy Kabins. The strata of civilization shows in the ways locals earn their living. Almost every town, no matter how small, employs a minister and a bartender. There are combination grocery/ hardware/ snack shops, an effort to consolidate and serve as many needs of the community as possible.

Some towns, usually those less than twelve blocks long, still look as they must have forty years ago. There are cafés, bars, hardware stores, a local grocer, a gas station, a church, a post office. No combination of the above is considered unreasonable. If you need more than that, it requires a trip to the nearest larger town. And there is usually someone who earns his or her living bringing goods from the next rung on the population ladder.

When traveling one of the more scenic highways, we always find a sprinkling of gift shops, or a sign advertising the local attempts at tourism - fishing guides, museums of regional consequence, river rafting tours. And there is the occasional rugged individual selling the unique, which is sometimes inspiring, sometimes tacky. There are Van Gogh reproductions, J.R.R. Tolkien figures of wax, lawn ornaments carved from driftwood, hand blown glassware, original pottery, and testimonials to local miracles to be found along the roadway. Opinions will differ on what is tacky and what is inspiring, but all of these entrepreneurs deserve points for creativity.

There are many decisions to be made about what deserves our attention during the journey along the road. A tourist often seeks out that which has been served up; safe, clean, and reliable. Often the carnival atmosphere of manmade tourist attractions is too glitzy to pass up. And our souls may need such presentations. They are uniquely American in flavor. They put us in touch with our cultural pathos.

But true travelers seek out what lies beyond, the natural sights which inspired the original explorers and the people and events which flowed from their discoveries.

A traveler may visit the museum of the local founding father, but also seeks out the lives of those who lived beneath his shadow and the lesser players who brought his dreams into reality. A traveler does not just rely upon the view of the wilderness presented by a slide show, but seeks out the forests for a personal experience. And although a meal at the local chain represents a part of our culture which cannot be ignored, a traveler knows that while food served by local chefs may not be as predictable, it is usually more representative of the place he came to see.

A traveler often gives the spirit equal representation with the body, knowing even bad food can make for good memories. The story is the thing, not just the flavor of the moment. Along American roads, many stories are unfolding to travelers, full of the lives of people who settled into a local vision.

On this trip, our destination was Eureka, California. But the road we took to get there, U.S. Highway 101, encompasses a true cross section of American culture. Ambling down the western coastline, from Canada to Los Angeles, this road is unconcerned about timetables or sensibilities. The blacktop itself is not old, but the origins of the highway date back to the mission trails blazed by friars in late 1700's. It is certainly among the most diverse of American roads, encompassing desert and foothills, steep cliffs and sandy beaches, ancient forests and modern vineyards. And because its rugged terrain has discouraged the wholesale use of pavement, U.S. 101 remains a passage with a wild and uncivilized view.

Driving down the coast from Canada, almost due south, the moon sets with gentle silence into the ocean over one shoulder as the sun rises in fierce glory over the other. Towering, mighty, rocky cliffs oversee the horizon along the Washington and Oregon coastlines. Spilling into the agitated sea, monoliths of rock stand unconcerned against the persistent waves which explode at their feet. The mountains and old growth forests keep their vigil in silence as they have for centuries.

Once into California, the coast gradually becomes less rugged. The harshness of unforgiving rocky crags is exchanged for the peace and quietude of statuesque redwood giants laden heavily with cool fog. To hurry by without notice of the forested landscape is to thumb your nose at health. Here, along the narrow, curving, diving roads, the titans stand so close to the road that you can see the nick marks in the bark from the bumpers of those who proceeded you. Few roads remind so vividly the wisdom of respect for nature.

The redwoods themselves are all they are described to be and more. Some of these trees are three thousand years old, twenty feet in diameter, and two hundred feet to the first limb. The trees have a thick bark that make them almost insect and fire resistant. They are trees of a moist, cool climate, so the coastal fogs of northern California suit them perfectly.

Halfway along U.S. 101, equidistant from its beginning in Los Angeles and its end in the brisk sound waters that separate Washington state from Canada, is Eureka, California. Heralding itself as the heart of the redwood forest, Eureka is a destination in itself. A slow growing, peaceful town, Eureka is a study in history.

Highway 101 did not come to Eureka until the early 1900's. Until then, the only way to get there was by boat, a twenty-two hour trip from San Francisco if the weather was good, a frighteningly endless one if you should encounter a storm.

Among the redwoods below Eureka, the highway turns away from the sea, and into a land of rolling hills, wooded mountains, and some of the best wine country in the world. This gives us the first sense that the highway was originally a mission trail. Wine was needed for the communal mass, so each mission planted its own vineyard, inadvertently founding California's wine industry. As we near San Francisco, the names that roll by as we traverse from town to town remind us of California's Spanish heritage.

Highway 101 travels right through San Francisco, a town sometimes referred to as "Everyone's Favorite City." Just a sleepy mission until the gold rush entered the scene, the city has a legendary mystique and boasts a colorful beginning which would shame most of the friars who founded the city.

The further south we travel on Highway 101, the more desertlike the terrain. The climate California is famous for becomes apparent as we leave the bay area and head toward the sunny shores of southern California. Many miles north of Los Angeles, U.S. 101 turns oceanward to hug the California coastline. Urban sprawl and eclectic lifestyles, surfers and beach bunnies, stunning oceanside residences and ranches, cypress and palm trees, all the things which comprise California's reputation become readily apparent now. To know L.A. is not necessarily to love it, but no one could ever deny that it is an interesting place.

To complete the trek of the west coast of the United States and travel into Mexico involves taking Interstate 5. Highway 101 ends, or begins depending on your perspective, at the City of Angels. If you have the time, this adventure is one worth taking. If time is a limitation, a trip to the Eureka area will encapsulate much of the experiences to be had along the entire length of Highway 101.

Northern California is a remote place. The area is heavily forested and often mountainous. Except for those towns which have sprung up along the highways which run from north to south in the state, there are few population centers of any size. The people who inhabit these towns are the descendants of pioneers; lumberjacks, farmers, trappers, fishermen, hunters, and gold miners. More recently, escapees from larger cities are looking for the quality of life that small town living brings. Rugged individualists, these people are independent and strong minded.

Of northern California's coastal counties, Humboldt is the most beautiful, overwhelmingly serene in some places, strikingly powerful in others. Filled with the kind of ideal small towns that many Americans would like to live in, the county is half a day's journey from San Francisco. The highway that connects these towns, 101, never reaches the county's southern coastal areas. The Kings Range, an area of formidable cliffs that rise several thousand feet straight up from the ocean, is so impassable that even a road as sinuous as Highway 101 could not get through. This is how the area came to be known as the lost coast.

The towns which dot Humboldt county, Eureka, Arcata, McKinleyville, Samoa, Garberville and Trinidad, to name a few, are more reminiscent of their Pacific Northwest neighbors than their Southern California relatives. Ancient forests, stretches of coarse sand, windswept beaches, pockets of family oriented communities, and mild Pacific Northwest weather surround these towns.

The small college in Arcata is progressive and provides the area with entertainment and culture that might not otherwise be available in so small and remote a place. The town also harbors a world famous bird sanctuary, famous because it is also a water treatment plant, an unusual and surprisingly workable combination of nature and human resources. The people of the county appreciate the college and it is one of the few areas where government and educators work hand in hand to improve the quality of life in the community.

Twelve miles south of Arcata, on Humboldt Bay, is Eureka. Many people who make a living in Eureka work with their hands, although that is as likely to mean they are artists as anything else. The county boasts the largest artist population per capita of any community in California. Of the remaining residents of Eureka, some work in the timber industry, some are fisherman, some are shipyard and railway workers, some are part of a growing retirement community, and some work in the hospitality industry.

With Highway 101 running through it's center, Eureka is difficult to miss. But if you do not venture off the beaten path, you might miss Eureka's spirit and charm. The rows of chain motels and restaurants which line 101 may be at the center of town, but they are not at its heart.

Just two blocks off the main highway are Carter House Inn and Hotel Carter, establishments that come much closer to representing the true nature of Eureka than ubiquitous hamburger chains. By journeying the two blocks from the main road to 3rd street, travelers find they have gone from a world of neon and the predictable, to a world of authenticity and the enduring. Both the inn and the hotel capture the sense of heritage, the genuineness, the style and quality that is Eureka at its best.

Innkeepers and owners, Mark and Christi Carter, have been called the "accidental" innkeepers because they never intended to be involved in the hospitality industry. But they are naturals for it, none the less. They are the kind of people who make you feel comfortable. It is not just that they smile a lot, but that their smiles are so sincere.

When we first met the Carters, we asked Mark if he was so good natured because he made a living doing what he wanted. He replied that he did not think of what he did as work, that it was simply his life. Perhaps that attitude is why he is always enjoying himself and why his enjoyment of life is contagious.

"We find we get an entirely different clientele here than the people who stay on the main road," Mark told us. "It is amazing how that two blocks draws out the adventurers. We like our clientele. They have a keen eye for what matters in life. They know how to enjoy themselves, and how to investigate."

The clientele certainly reflect the hosts, for that description fits Mark and Christi. Mark Carter is an adventurer. Not the kind who blazes trails through the wilderness or scales mountain peaks, but the type who restores cities and challenges outmoded economic theories. He is neither a dull guy, nor a flashy politician, but something of a loveable maverick. When you meet him, you will certainly notice his warm, friendly manner and the mischievous gleam in his eyes.

Mark was born and raised in Eureka. His father and mother were a strong presence in the community. Twice when we were out on the street with Mark, Eureka natives came over to chat with him and comment on how much they missed his parents. The elder Carters passed away only a few years ago. Mark was not hesitant to tell us he missed them too. They provided him with vision, determination, and confidence. He speaks fondly of his parents.

Christi, Mark's wife, laughingly told us that she thought Mark might have been a bit of a rowdy, if it had not been for his loving, supportive parents.

"Actually, that is what brought us together," Christi told us, "We both liked our parents. That may sound funny, but after having so many friends who had difficult childhoods, I was impressed when I met a man who spoke so highly of his family."

Mark and Christi met in one of the areas earthy bars. Mark describes it as the kind of place where you can tell what time of day it is by the crowd present. There are business people at lunch, college students in the afternoon, singles after work, and bikers late at night. He did not tell us, however, what time of day he met Christi there.

Christi was a student at Humboldt State College at the time though, so that might give us an idea. A home economics major seeking a degree in textiles and design, she soon found the college provided little in that area. She found herself gravitating toward chefdom, an early hint of the Carter House's legend.

Mark was a builder when they met. When he was young, only 10 years old, his father had told him about a man who had built several buildings in town and who now lived off the income from his property. Mark's father pointed out how the man was free to spend his time doing anything he wanted. Even at such a young age, Mark thought, "That's for me."

After a short try at architectural school, Mark left college to become a builder. He brought a keen sense of quality and a fascination with design into his work. Later, after he and Christi married, they renovated a row of buildings and opened an ice cream parlor in one of the shops.

"I really did not know what I was getting into," Christi confides. "I thought I would make a simple lunch, dish out a little ice cream, make a few pastries. How hard could it be? After the first month, I was ready to quit."

"What kept you going?" we asked.

"Mark's parents. They always seemed to know when things were not going well. They would come get us, take us out to eat, tell us how proud they were of us and how great they thought we were. By the time they took us home, we were ready to try again. And Mark's mother amazed me with the wonderful pastries she would make to help out. I learned a lot from her."

At the same time Mark was building and refurbishing buildings, Eureka was remodeling its old town area. The remoteness of the town has spared it the boom and bust mentality which plagues other parts of the state. But it has also meant slow economic and population growth. This has been a blessing to Eureka because it has not paved over its heritage. It is one of the few towns we have visited that still has lovely, viable residential neighborhoods downtown, scattered among the offices and shops of the business district.

Eureka can proudly point to houses that were built in the Victorian era, the nineteen twenties, the thirties, and the post war era, all beautifully maintained and occupied. These houses exist not as museum pieces, but as living, workable parts of the community. But it is the Victorians for which Eureka has become known. And it was the Victorian style which began to capture Mark Carter's imagination. Before he knew it, he was involved in an urban renewal project, helping people rethink the spread to the suburb mentality and refocus on inhabiting livable cities.

He and Christi decided they wanted to build an authentic Victorian as their dream house. They chose to build the house right downtown, not out in the suburbs. They found the exact plan they wanted in an old pattern book from the turn of the century. The house had been designed by Samuel and Joseph Newsom, the architects of Eureka's, indeed, the western United States's, best known Victorian, the Carson Mansion. Built for a San Francisco family, the house Mark wanted to replicate had been destroyed in the 1906 earthquake.

Mark and three assistants went to work on the house immediately, and finished it in 16 months. Most people who visit Carter House cannot believe the building has not been there for years, even though the only old things built into the house are a pair of brass hinges and two sinks. As one guest told Mark, "I know construction and this is too well built to be new." But the house is actually an updated Victorian, true to every detail in construction, but light, spacious, bright, and warm inside. The white walls hold no wallpaper, the polished oak floors and handsome woodwork provide architectural interest. Mark takes great personal pride in all his projects. He even made his own moldings so he could get them just right for the house.

But there were problems along the way. The project cost three times what they estimated and interest rates doubled during the building process. And while they thought they had adequate furnishings for the four story house, when they moved in, they found the rooms almost bare.

To help finance the house, Mark and Christi opened an antique shop on the first floor. They always had been strong supporters of the art community, so they also began to display the paintings of local artists. A few overnight guests made their way to Mark and Christi's home and they realized, perhaps before the Carters did, the potential of the house.

Having people in their home turned out to be an experience the Carters found enjoyable and rewarding. They discovered that they liked being innkeepers and expanded their idea of taking in a few overnight guests into a bed and breakfast. Eventually, demand for their rooms became so great that Mark and Christi moved their family out of the house and gave the entire 6500 square feet over to the guests.

By now, Christi's reputation as a chef was spreading fast. California magazine called the four course Carter House breakfast the best in the state. National magazines sent writers to find out what the fuss was about. Word of mouth brought friends of former guests and relatives of local residents to visit. Even visitors from San Francisco, a mecca of fine dining, were impressed with Christi's creations.

The Carters, faced with more business than they had ever imagined, opened a hotel across the street from Carter House to handle the overflow of guests. The hotel, an intimate 20 rooms, is built with the same care and decorated with the same homeyness and warmth that have made the Carter House reputation. And the hotel offers not only breakfast, but an astounding dinner menu as well.

Mark and Christi are modest about their accomplishments. "We have a great staff," Christi told us. "They are interesting people, they like the public, they are talented and adventurous. They make the Carter reputation as much as we do."

Meanwhile, the Carters continue to stay busy. Christi does volunteer work at the school. Their children, Joseph and Annie, are the center of her life at the moment. They still showcase the work of local artists and support the community in its renewal efforts. And Mark has given life to another Victorian. In spite of that, they still find time to mingle with the guests at the afternoon hors d'oeuvres and wine served by the hotel, and Christi still experiments with new ideas for the Carter kitchens. It was a lucky accident for Eureka and its guests that the Carters stumbled, however unintentionally, into the travel business. We look forward to their next endeavor with anticipation. For now we are content with Christi's recipes and ideas.

—Denise & Michael Shumway
The Traveling Gourmets

The Carter style began at Carter House. Many of our first guests were business travelers and I felt I had to serve more than juice and a muffin to keep them coming back.

I planned substantial menus because I was not sure how many opportunities these busy travelers had to eat during the day. And, because I enjoyed pastries so much, I added them to the main course. Within a short time, the Carter House multi-course breakfast evolved.

In this chapter of breakfast recipes, I have included several recipes from each of our courses; fruits, muffins, main and side dishes. If you want to impress guests with a spectacular breakfast or brunch, just choose one dish from each category. I leave it to you to pick your favorites for personalized menus.

At Hotel Carter, we set up a buffet table for breakfast with lots of pastries, cereals, fruits, and juices. Several of those pastry recipes are included in the dessert chapter, but are excellent for breakfast. And, of course, several of the breakfast recipes would work well at dinner.

Many of these recipes are written to be adapted for few or many guests. For that reason, those recipes do not tell you how many people they serve.

Recipes throughout the book contain sauces which you may want to use in other dishes. I have separated the sauce ingredients at the top of the recipe so you can easily know which are needed to make it. The instructions are incorporated in the recipe at the most convenient time for making the sauce, but the sauce instructions are marked by an underlined bullet ●, so you can separate the sauce instructions from the rest of the recipe.

- Christi

Poached Pears in Zinfandel Sauce

A simple, yet tasty and uncommon dish. A fine way to elevate any meal to a "beyond the pale" status.

1 pear per person
1 quart Zinfandel wine
1 cup granulated sugar
1 dozen cloves
1 Tablespoon cinnamon
juice of 1 1/2 lemons
1 teaspoon nutmeg
sprigs of mint and apple, cherry, or pear blossoms,
    for garnish

- Place the wine, sugar, cloves, cinnamon, lemon juice, and nutmeg in a large cooking pot. Mix ingredients well, then bring to a boil.
- Peel and half the pears. Place pear halves into the boiling wine mixture and cook until they are tender. Remove the pears.
- Continue boiling the wine mixture until it reduces to a fine syrup consistency. Remove the mixture from the heat and strain through a fine screen.
- Place pears on individual serving plates. Cover each with wine sauce. Garnish with a sprig of mint and a fruit blossom.

A ripe peach, pear, plum, melon, tomato, or avacado should yield a little to gentle pressure while still feeling firm. You can recognize ripeness in tree fruits and melons by their smell. Fully ripened fruits produce a fragrance that adds to their taste.

- Christi

The rule for traveling abroad is to take our common sense with us, and leave our prejudices behind.
... William Hazlitt

Apple Fritters

These apple fritters are beautiful, scrumptious and easy to prepare. What more could you ask?

The word fritter derives, like all good culinary words, from French - in this case middle French, friture - and means to fry. Apple fritter in French is pommes frites.

A good piece of fruit will be heavy for its size.

2 apples
2 cups flour
1 Tablespoon sugar
1/2 teaspoon salt
1 bottle beer (12 ounces)
2 egg whites, whipped
vegetable oil
2 cups whipped cream

- Mix the flour, sugar and salt. Pour in the beer and mix until smooth.
- Fold in the whipped egg whites. Set batter in the refrigerator for at least 30 minutes.
- Cut the apples into thin slices. In a frying pan, heat at least 1 inch of oil to 375°. Dip the apple slices in the batter, coating generously, then place them in the oil for about 2 minutes, or until golden brown. Remove fritters and place on a paper towel to drain.
- Serve with whipped cream.

Makes 20 to 30 fritters.

Adam and Eve had many advantages, but the principle one was that they escaped teething.
... Mark Twain

Sautéed Plums

1 ripe plum per person
1/2 cup granulated sugar
2/3 cup white wine
1/4 teaspoon black pepper, freshly ground
1/4 teaspoon nutmeg
1/4 cup butter, (1/2 cube)

Plums are a summer
fruit and can be found
in the market June
through September.
Plums freeze with only
fair quality.

- Half plums and remove the pits.
- In a sauté pan, combine the wine and sugar. Cook over low heat until the sugar dissolves.
- Melt butter and add to the mixture.
- Place plums into the pan, insides down, skin sides up. Cook until the fruit is tender, but not mushy.
- Remove plums. Add pepper and nutmeg to the pan and stir well. Continue cooking sauce until it reduces down to approximately half its original volume.
- Serve plums bathed in sauce.

In Italy, edible flowers
are often dipped into
crêpe or fritter batter,
then fried in deep fat.
When sprinkled with
sugar, they are crunchy
and full of flavor as well
as quite colorful.
Nasturtiums make
beautiful and tasty
fritters.

Strawberries Romanoff

1 basket fresh strawberries, washed and sliced into
   quarters
3 ounces Gran Marnier
3 ounces Kirsch
1/4 cup sugar
1 cup heavy cream, whipped to a soft peak
mint sprigs and pansy blooms, for garnish

- Combine strawberries, Gran Marnier, Kirsch and sugar in a bowl. Let the mixture marinate in the refrigerator for 15 minutes.
- Drain marinade from the strawberries and gently fold fruit into the whipped cream.
- Serve in parfait dishes garnished with mint sprigs and pansy blooms.

Serves 4.

Few fruits are as versatile in the kitchen as strawberries. They freeze well, can be used in ice-creams, sherbets, parfaits, pies, sauces, and jams. Their bright color and sweet aroma add to any plate. An excellent dessert is fresh strawberries dipped in melted chocolate.

- Christi

A ripe strawberry is deep red in color and shiny.

Morning Glory Muffins

2 cups all purpose flour
1 cup sugar
2 teaspoons baking powder
1 teaspoon cinnamon
1 teaspoon nutmeg
1 apple, peeled, cored and grated
1/2 cup raisins
1/2 cup coconut, shredded
1/2 cup pecans, chopped
1 cup carrot, grated
3 eggs
1 cup vegetable oil
2 teaspoons real vanilla extract

- Grease and flour 24 muffin tins. Preheat the oven to 350°.
- Sift flour, sugar, baking powder, cinnamon, and nutmeg into a large mixing bowl. Add the grated apple, raisins, coconut, pecans, and carrot. Mix together thoroughly, until the mixture resembles a coarse meal.
- In a separate bowl, beat the eggs slightly and add the vegetable oil and vanilla extract. Pour the wet ingredients into the dry ingredients and quickly combine. Fill the muffin tins with the batter until they are 3/4 full.
- Bake for 20 to 25 minutes or until the muffins are golden brown.

Makes 24 muffins.

When doubling a baking recipe, do not double the salt.

I recommend being careful about not filling the muffin tins too full and making huge muffins. If other foods are being served with the bread, you do not want your guests to spoil their appetites on the muffins. And the smaller ones are more helathy and more appetizing as a snack or in a lunch.

--Christi

Apple/Raisin Muffins

2 1/2 cups flour
3/4 cup sugar
1 Tablespoon baking powder
3/4 cup heavy cream
1/4 cup fresh lemon juice
1/2 cup vegetable oil
2 eggs, slightly beaten
1 cup shredded Granny Smith apple
1/2 cup small golden raisins

- Grease and flour 24 muffin tins. Preheat the oven to 350°.
- Sift flour, sugar, and baking powder into a mixing bowl.
- Make a well in the center of the powdered ingredients and add cream, lemon juice, vegetable oil, and eggs. Mix until loosely combined.
- Add shredded apple and golden raisins.
- Fill greased muffin tins 3/4 full with batter and bake 20 to 30 minutes or until golden brown.

Makes 24 muffins.

In 1975, Kent Whealy started Seed Savers Exchange, an organization that aspires to save some of the world's rare species of plants. The world's staple food supply depends on fewer than two dozen species of plants. Ancient plant forebears developed in a particular home of origin. Ethiopia is the motherland of barley and coffee. The Mediterranean gave us asparagus, beets, cabbage, lettuce, oats, and olives. From Asia Minor came alfalfa, rye, lentils, almonds, apricots, apples, and pears. Southwest Asia gave us wheat. And India and Burma provided rice, yams, and cucumbers.

Cheddar Cheese Muffins

2 cups flour
3 Tablespoons sugar
3 teaspoons baking powder
1/2 teaspoon salt
3 Tablespoons butter, softened
1 cup milk
1 egg
1 1/2 cups cheddar cheese, grated
1/2 cup powdered sugar, for dusting

- Grease and flour 24 muffin tins. Preheat the oven to 400°.
- Mix flour, baking powder, sugar, and salt in a medium size bowl. Set aside.
- Put egg, milk, and butter into a food processor. Cover and process until the mixture is smooth. Stir in the grated cheese.
- Pour the wet ingredients into the dry ingredients and combine until the mixture is just moistened.
- Spoon batter into greased muffin cups and bake for 20 to 25 minutes. Dust with powdered sugar before serving.

Makes 24 muffins.

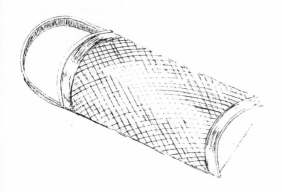

The origins of cheese date back to about 9,000 B.C., when animals were first domesticated. There are many legends about how cheese was created and many countries claim to have invented it. Here is our favorite cheese legend.

In ancient Sumeria a traveling merchant filled his shoulder bag with fresh milk. Bags in those days were made from the stomach of a calf. He set off on a long arduous journey with few rest stops. When he stopped for dinner that night, he found to his dismay that the contents of his primitive canteen had solidified. Not having anything else to eat, he cut open his bag and consumed the solid lumpy food. To his delight, it was delicious. In modern times, we know that the rennet naturally present in the stomach lining of a young animal, combined with the heat and movement of the days journey, had separated the milk. No doubt the excited merchant returned home to present his new food to an eager marketplace.

Chocolate Cheesecake Muffins

for cream cheese filling:
3 ounces cream cheese
2 Tablespoons sugar

for muffins:
1 1/2 cup flour
4 1/2 Tablespoons unsweetened cocoa
1/2 cup sugar
1 Tablespoon baking powder
1/2 teaspoon salt
2 eggs, beaten
1 cup milk
1/2 cup oil
1 cup powdered sugar, for dusting

- Grease 12 muffin tins. Preheat oven to 375°.
- In a small bowl, blend cream cheese and sugar until fluffy. Set aside.
- In a large bowl, mix well the flour, cocoa, sugar, baking powder, and salt. Create a well in the center of the dry mixture.
- In a separate bowl, combine milk, egg, and oil. Add liquid mixture all at once to the dry ingredients, stirring until quite moist. Batter should be quite lumpy.
- Spoon about 1 Tablespoon of batter into each muffin cup. Drop 1 teaspoon cream cheese or top of each half-filled muffin cup, then fill with more batter until 3/4 full.
- Bake muffins for twenty minutes. Dust with powdered sugar before serving.

Makes a baker's dozen muffins.

The term baker's dozen originated in the days when bread was the diet's main staple. There were severe penalties for any baker who short weighted a loaf of bread. To be sure to cover themselves, bakers added an extra loaf to every twelve sold to the market. Thus a baker's dozen is thirteen rather than twelve.

Orange Tea Muffins

for topping:
3 Tablespoons sugar
1/3 cup orange juice

for muffins:
1 1/2 cup flour
1/2 cup sugar
2 teaspoons baking powder
1/2 teaspoon salt
1/2 cup butter
1/2 cup orange juice
2 eggs
rind of 1 orange, grated
1/4 cup powdered sugar

- Grease 12 muffin tins. Preheat the oven to 375°.
- Combine sugar and orange juice for the topping and set aside.
- Combine flour, sugar, baking powder, and salt. Blend well and set aside.
- Melt the butter. Remove melted butter from the heat and stir in the orange juice, eggs, and orange rind. Beat well.
- Combine liquid ingredients with the dry mixture and blend until the mixture is just moistened. Set aside 1/2 cup of the batter, then spoon the remaining batter into the muffin tins.
- Mix the topping mixture with the 1/2 cup of remaining batter. Spoon a little of the mixture on the top of each muffin.
- Bake muffins for 15 to 20 minutes.
- Sprinkle with powdered sugar and serve.

Makes 12 muffins.

Recipe for cowboy coffee:
Place 1 Tablespoon of coffee per cup of water, or a handful of coffee for a gallon pot of water, into a flour or sugar sack, cottton sock, or jean's leg and tie firmly. Add to boiling water and remove from the fire when the brew is strong enough, from 3 -5 minutes. Slowly add cold water to settle the grounds. Serve straight or laced with cream and sugar.

Eggs Jerusalem with Orange Champagne Sauce

for Eggs Jerusalem:
2 large artichokes
1 lemon, halved
2 small carrots
salt and pepper, to taste
2 eggs
1 teaspoon chives

for Orange Champagne Sauce:
1/2 cup freshly squeezed orange juice
1/2 cup champagne
1/4 pound (1 stick) unsalted butter, melted

The edible part of the artichoke is the flower of the plant. Artichokes are not from the Middle East, but Italy.

I dislike feeling at home when I'm abroad.
... George Bernard Shaw

- Bring a large pot of water to a boil. Cut the stems off the artichokes and discard them. Rub the artichoke with the halved lemon. Cut off the top leaves just above the choke and discard them. Rub the tops of the artichoke with lemon.
- Squeeze the remaining lemon juice into the boiling water and add the artichokes. Boil artichokes for about 25 minutes or until the bottoms can be easily pierced with a knife.
- Cook the carrots in lightly salted water until tender.
- While the artichokes and carrots are cooking, make the sauce. In a heavy saucepan, combine the orange juice and champagne. Reduce the liquid until it becomes a glaze, roughly 3/4 its original volume.
- Remove the pan from the heat and whisk butter into the liquid, 2 Tablespoons at a time. Return the pan to the heat each time you add 2 Tablespoons of butter and whisk it in until all the butter is incorporated. The sauce

should have the consistency of Hollandaise when it is finished. Set sauce aside in a warm place.

- Cut the carrots and purée in a food processor. Remove the carrot purée.
- Cool the cooked artichokes by running cool water over them. Remove the remaining leaves and chokes and trim the hearts flat.
- Spoon carrot purée onto the artichoke hearts. Place the hearts on a plate in a slightly warm oven.
- Bring another pan of water to a boil. Remove the pan of water from the heat and poach 2 eggs in the water for 3 to 4 minutes.
- Remove eggs from the water and place on artichoke hearts over carrot purée. Spoon the champagne sauce over the egg and artichoke and garnish with chives.

Serves 2.

True Champagne is made only in France, in the small area around the city of Reims. No other sparkling wine has the right to use the name, even though many do. Americans use the name freely, but the Italians call their sparkling wines Spumantè. In Germany sparkling white wine is called Sekt.

Champagne is costly because making it involves expensive time and labor. Every bottle is fitted with a temporary cork and then stored neck down in a slanted position for many months. A slight turn is given to each bottle, two or three times per week, so that the impurities produced by fermentation will settle around the cork. Eventually the cork is removed, taking the impurities with it. A small amount of sugar syrup is added, the bottle is recorked, wired, sealed, and stored for a year or more.

Fresh Corn Waffles with Cilantro Butter

Like no other waffle you have eaten.

Waffle batter:
1 cup all-purpose flour
1/2 cup yellow corn meal
2 Tablespoons sugar
2 teaspoons double-acting baking powder
1/4 teaspoon salt
1 large egg
2 Tablespoons melted unsalted butter
1/2 cup water
1 cup fresh corn, removed from cob just before
    adding
1 teaspoon real vanilla extract
vegetable oil

Cilantro butter:
1/4 pound softened sweet butter
1/4 cup fresh cut cilantro

When serving waffles or pancakes, please treat yourself and your guests with kindness and use real maple syrup. It does make a difference.
- Christi

- In a large bowl, mix together flour, corn meal, sugar, baking powder, and salt.
- In a separate large bowl, whip together egg, melted butter, water, corn, and vanilla.
- Add egg mixture to flour mixture and mix until just combined.
- Heat and oil waffle iron, and cook waffle according to manufacturer's specifications.
- Whip cilantro and butter together until smooth and creamy.
- Top each waffle with cilantro butter and serve with real maple syrup.

Poached Eggs with Asiago Cheese Sauce

for Asiago Cheese Sauce:
2 Tablespoons unsalted butter
2 Tablespoons all purpose flour
1/2 cup chicken broth
1/2 cup heavy cream
1/2 cup (2 ounces) Asiago cheese, grated

for eggs:
4 slices sweet Virginia ham
2 English muffins, split and buttered
4 eggs
freshly ground pepper
fresh herb sprigs and pansies, for garnish

- In a small saucepan, melt the butter. Blend in the flour. Stir over medium high heat for 1 minute.
- Whisk in chicken broth and cream. Cook, whisking constantly, until thickened and bubbly. Whisk in cheese until melted. Cover the sauce and set aside in a warm place.
- On a baking sheet, arrange ham slices on English muffin halves. Broil 3 inches from heat for 2 minutes. Keep warm.
- Bring 1/2 inch of water to boiling in a large skillet. Reduce heat. Slip eggs into the water. Simmer 4 to 6 minutes. Baste yolks with simmering water.
- Remove eggs from the water with a slotted spoon and arrange over ham and muffins.
- Pour sauce over each egg. Sprinkle with freshly ground pepper. Garnish with fresh herb sprigs and pansies.

Serves 4.

When serving a dish with poached eggs, you can make the eggs ahead of time, then keep them in cold water. This is especially helpful when poaching eggs for a large number of people. When you are ready to serve the eggs just emerse them for a few minutes in hot water to warm them.

- Mark

Eggs are called poached because of the white pouch which surrounds the yolk when the egg is cooked.

Frittata with Dijon-Hollandaise Sauce

This delicious frittata will ruin you for "regular" omelets forever!

A frittata is an Italian omelet. The difference between a frittata and a basic omelet is that the filling is mixed with the eggs before they are poured into the pan. A frittata is always served flat. Generally the top has been sprinkled with grated cheese and the frittata is often broiled under direct heat for a couple of seconds. Frittatas are excellent for use with leftovers, whether they are vegetables, fruits, meat, or fish.

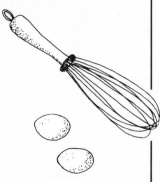

for Frittata:
8 ounces cream cheese
1/2 cup flour
1 dozen eggs
1 red onion
5 cloves garlic
3 zucchinis
4 chanterelle mushrooms
1 yellow sweet pepper
1/4 cup fresh basil leaves, chopped and loosely
 packed
1/4 pound Swiss cheese, grated
3/4 teaspoon salt
1/4 teaspoon white pepper

for Dijon-Hollandaise Sauce:
3 egg yolks
2 dashes white pepper
1 dash cayenne pepper
1/2 cube unsalted butter
juice of 1/2 lemon
1/4 teaspoon salt
2 Tablespoons coarse grain Dijon mustard

- Grease a 12 inch tart pan with removable bottom. Preheat the oven to 300°.
- Whip together cream cheese, flour, and 4 eggs. Set aside.
- Chop finely, process, or grate: red onion, garlic, zucchinis, chanterelle mushrooms, yellow sweet pepper, and fresh basil leaves. Place mixture into a cloth napkin and squeez out all excess moisture. Then place mixture into large mixing bowl.

- To the cream cheese mixture, add 8 more eggs, the grated Swiss cheese, salt, and white pepper. Whip together well.
- Add cheese and egg mixture to mixing bowl of chopped vegetables. Blend well.
- Pour batter into the prepared pan. Bake at 300° for 1 hour.
- Just before the frittata comes out of the oven, prepare the sauce. In a double boiler, whip egg yolks and lemon juice until the mixture has a custard-like consistency. Add salt, white pepper, and cayenne pepper.
- In a separate pan, melt butter, then add it very slowly, a few drops at a time, to the egg yolk mixture, whipping constantly. Add mustard and blend well.
- Top frittata with Dijon Hollandaise Sauce.

Serves 6.

Never argue at the dinner table, for the one who is not hungry always gets the best of the argument.
... Richard Whately

An emulsion is the combination of two basically incompatible liquids such as oil and water. When combining them, an emulsifying agent such as an egg yolk is necessary. In hollandaise the egg yolk binds together the incompatible butter (oil) and the lemon juice (water). As the oil is beaten, it is broken down into tiny drops which spread evenly through the water. Adding the egg yolk combines the two. An emulsified mixture, such as French dressing, will separate easily without an emulsifying agent.

Poached Egg in Puff Pastry with Spinach Pancetta Sauce

This is one of those dishes that re-invents breakfast.

The recipe for puff pastry can be found on page 117.
This dough freezes very well, so I like to make it ahead of time and use it over a period of weeks for a variety of dishes.

Frozen puff pastry dough is available from your grocer's freezer. Making puff pastry is fun, and I recommend that everyone try it once, but it is very time consuming. For those of you on busy schedules, the frozen variety is delicious and easy to work with.

- Christi

for Egg in Puff Pastry:
puff pastry dough
6 large eggs
egg wash (2 eggs and 1 Tablespoon of water beat together)
Asiago cheese, for garnishing

for Spinach Pancetta Sauce:
1 cup white wine
1 yellow onion
6 cloves garlic
2 cups heavy cream
3 bunches fresh spinach
1/4 pound pancetta, chopped

- Make puff pastry dough. Cut dough into 5 inch squares of 1/4 inch thickness.
- Poach the eggs. Set aside.
- Chop onion and garlic. Place in a saucepan with wine and reduce over high heat until just 1 Tablespoon of liquid remains. Add 2 cups of cream and reduce over low heat until 1 cup of sauce remains.
- Lightly steam 3 bunches of fresh spinach. Place steamed spinach in food processor and purée with 1/4 cup of the cream sauce until the mixture is smooth. Add the remaining cream sauce and process well.
- Strain the sauce through fine mesh.
- Pan fry 1/4 pound of chopped pancetta. Drain the fat. Add pancetta to spinach sauce. Set sauce aside in a warm place.
- Preheat oven to 375°. Take each 5 inch square of pastry dough and cut a 4 inch square out

of the center, leaving 5 inch "frames." Using water as glue, place 2 opposite corners of the frame onto 2 opposite corners of the removed 4 inch square, lining up the sides right on top of each other. Twist the other corners of the frame once so that it sits squarely on top of the square.

- Brush egg wash onto puff pastry shells and bake in the oven for about 20 minutes or until golden brown.
- Collapse centers of the pastries with the bottom of a ladle. Fill ladle dents with poached eggs. Cover egg puff pastries with spinach sauce, garnish with grated Asiago cheese and serve.

Serves 6.

Puff pastry is made of many thin layers of dough. The name, pâte feuilletèe, comes from the French words for pastry and leaf.

To make the layers, the pastry is folded, rolled, then chilled, over and over again. Each folding and rolling is called a turn.

Puff pastry is always baked before being filled because filling would prevent rising.

Do you know the difference between education and experience? Education is when you read the fine print; experience is what you get when you don't.

... Pete Seeger

Eggs Florentine with Asiago Cheese Sauce

for Eggs Florentine:
6 eggs, perfectly poached
3 English Muffins
1/4 cup butter
2 bunches fresh spinach
1/2 teaspoon nutmeg
salt and white pepper, to taste

for Asiago Cheese Sauce:
2 scallions, finely chopped (white parts only)
1/2 cup white wine
4 cloves garlic, finely minced
1/2 cup Asiago cheese
1 cup heavy cream

- In a saucepan, combine garlic, scallions, and wine. Reduce sauce over medium high heat until wine is almost gone.
- Add the cream and reduce again until the mixture thickens noticeably.
- Add the Asiago cheese and combine well. Keep sauce in a warm place until needed.
- Slice and toast muffins and spread with butter.
- Wilt spinach in a frying pan with fresh butter. Add salt and pepper to taste and sprinkle with approximately 1/4 teaspoon of nutmeg.
- Place spinach atop the buttered muffins. Lay poached eggs on top of the spinach. Cover with the cream sauce. Sprinkle with salt, pepper, and nutmeg before serving.

Serves 3.

Vegetable Omelet in Puff Pastry

for omelet:
puff pastry dough
5 fresh eggs
1 cup heavy cream
1/4 cup onions, chopped
1/2 cup spinach, chopped
1/3 cup red bell peppers, chopped
1/3 cup zucchini, chopped
1/8 cup ricotta cheese

for Hollandaise Sauce:
3 egg yolks
2 dashes white pepper
1 dash cayenne pepper
1/2 cube unsalted butter
juice of 1/2 lemon
1/4 teaspoon salt

- Preheat oven to 350°. Lightly grease a large tart pan.
- Take a circular cut-out of pastry dough and lay it on the bottom of the pan so that it conforms to the pan and reaches up the sides.
- Whip together eggs and cream. Top the dough with egg/cream mixture. Add onions, spinach, peppers, zucchini, and cheese.
- Place another layer of puff pastry over the top of these ingredients and form a pouch around the filling. Bake for 30 minutes.
- In a double boiler, whip egg yolks and lemon juice until the mixture has a custard-like consistency. Add salt and both peppers.
- In a separate pan, melt butter and add it slowly to the mixture, whipping constantly.
- When the pastry is removed from the oven, cover it with Hollandaise sauce and serve.

To prevent bacon from curling while frying, dip the strips into cold water before cooking.

Foods that make up for nutritional lapses:
While no food can do it all, the combination of a few ultra-nutritious ingredients over a few days can make up for times when your meals are not as healthy as they should be. Having the following foods over the period of a week helps keep your diet balanced:
Broccoli
Brussel Sprouts
Cabbage
Cantelope
Carrots
Dark Greens
Dried Beans
Non-fat Milk
Non-fat Yogurt
Grain Cereal
Salmon
Sweet Potatoes
Citrus Fruits
Whole Grain Bread

Shrimp / Spinach / Cheese Turnovers with Sherry Wine Cream Sauce

for turnovers:
puff pastry
fresh spinach leaves, stems removed, 2 per turnover
fresh bay shrimp, 3 ounces per turnover
ricotta or cream cheese
Asiago cheese
nutmeg
white pepper

for Sherry Wine Cream Sauce:
1 ounce sherry
3 ounces white wine
1 shallot, diced
1 clove garlic, diced
1 cup heavy cream
pinch of nutmeg
pinch of white pepper

- Preheat oven to 350°.
- Take squares of puff pastry and lay 2 spinach leaves on top of each one. Onto the leaves, place 3 ounces of shrimp and cover with ricotta or cream cheese and Asiago cheese. Sprinkle white pepper and a dash of nutmeg over each turnover.
- Wet the edges of each puff pastry square. Fold the dough over and seal the filling inside each turnover. Place the turnovers on the baking sheet.
- Bake for 30 minutes or until the turnovers are golden brown.
- In a saucepan over high heat, combine sherry, wine, shallot, and garlic. Reduce until liquid is almost evaporated.
- Diminish heat slightly and add cream.

Reduce sauce until it thickens nicely.
● Strain sauce to remove garlic and shallot pieces. Sprinkle sauce with nutmeg and white pepper.
● Just before serving, place the turnovers on individual serving dishes and pour the sauce over each one.

Carrots in Brandy Cream and Nutmeg

6 julienne carrots, thinly sliced
1/2 cup cream
2 ounces brandy
1 Tablespoon nutmeg
1/8 Tablespoon white pepper
1/8 Tablespoon salt
1/3 cup real maple syrup

Most of the vitamins in carrots are near the skin, so it is best to remove as little skin as possible. If the carrots are young and fresh, simply scrub them instead of peeling.

● Blanch carrots.
● Place carrots in a sauté pan with cream, brandy, nutmeg, pepper, salt, and syrup. Cook mixture over low heat until cream thickens. Carrots should remain firm. Serve immediately.
Serves 4.

Fresh Corn Off The Cobb

fresh corn, stripped from 4 large ears
1/3 cup champagne vinegar
1/4 cup extra virgin olive oil
1 cup bell peppers, diced
1/3 cup fresh chives, chopped
salt and pepper, to taste

The United States is the native home of pecans, blueberries, strawberries, cranberries, Concord grapes, and sunflowers. The corn and pumpkin squash that American Indians gave the Pilgrims came from Mexico and Central America. Tomatoes and potatoes originated in the Peruvian Andes.

- In a sauté pan, mix together ingredients and warm over medium low heat for about 5 minutes. Mixture does not need to be fully cooked. Serve immediately.

Serves 4.

It took the potato 200 years to reach its present popularity. Today potatoes are considered a staple of the diet and are a favorite side dish.

Morning Potatoes

1/2 potato per person
green and red bell peppers
garlic
onion
butter
salt and pepper
fresh rosemary and parsley, finely chopped

- Peel the potatoes and slice into cubic strips about 2 inches long.
- Blanch potato strips with garlic, salt, and pepper until just tender.
- Chop onions and bell peppers into small cubes. Sauté onions in butter until soft, then toss in bell peppers. Cook for 1 minute.
- When potatoes are done, strain off the water and toss into the pan with onions and peppers. Gently warm.
- Sprinkle parsley and rosemary over top of potatoes. Serve.

Fresh Spaghetti Squash

1 whole spaghetti squash
1/3 cup extra virgin olive oil
1/4 cup champagne vinegar
1 Tablespoon black pepper, freshly ground
1 teaspoon salt
1/3 cup fresh tarragon, diced

- Preheat oven to 350°.
- Slice squash in half lengthwise and scoop out the seeds. Place a small amount of water in the baking pan and place squash, meat side down, in the pan to bake. Bake for 30 minutes or until meat is tender.
- When squash is fully cooked, scoop the squash meat from the shell and place in a sauté pan with olive oil, vinegar, salt, pepper, and tarragon. Mix the ingredients well.
- Warm the mixture over medium low heat. Serve immediately.

Serves 4.

Squash is a large plant family which includes numerous varieties: summer squash, yellow crookneck, butternut, and pumpkins. Squash is very nutritious and can be prepared in a large variety of ways, including baking, steaming, and frying. Even the seeds are edible and when dried and salted are good snacks for people and birds.

May you have warmth in your igloo, oil in your lamp, and peace in your heart.
... Eskimo Proverb

Meats and Cheeses

As the world grows smaller, what was once exotic becomes commonplace. Arugula, tabbouleh, sushi, brie, phyllo, these foods were new to the American palate not many years ago. And new foods are being added to the menu every day. Here are a few meats and cheeses making their way into the American diet. Delis and ethnic food stores are the best places to shop for these delicacies.

Cheeses:

Asiago - originally made from sheep's milk, now from cow's milk. The young cheese is sometimes bitter, the aged version is mellower.

Chevre - cheese made from goat's milk. There are many kinds, from cheddar to feta to mozzarella. All can be used like the corresponding cow cheeses. Fresh chevres hold their shape when they melt.

Mascarpone - an Italian cheese with a fresh, rich, buttery flavor.

Gorgonzola - Italian blue cheese; sweet, creamy, pungent. When aged, it is dry and crumbly. It is called blue because of the characteristic blue-green veins created when flavor producing molds are injected during the curing process.

Stilton - England's premier blue cheese.

Roquefort - France's best know blue, made from sheep's milk.

Gruyère - firm Swiss with small holes and a sweet, nutty flavor.

Jarlsberg - slightly sweet, slightly waxy, a firm cheese from Norway.

Meats:

Pancetta - Italian bacon, cured but not smoked. Available in ethnic food stores and occasionally in the deli section of the supermarket.

Prosciutto - an aged, air dried ham which is cured in a spicy brine. This meat is called parma ham in Italy.

Escabeche - pickled fish from South America.

Carpaccio - extra thin slices of lightly seared beef or fish.

Chorizo - spicy Spanish sausage, used in many Mexican dishes.

Cabrito - goat.

Grousse - partridge.

Squab - young tender pigeons that have been farm raised.

Eureka History and Architecture

The factor which most shaped Eureka's heritage is its isolation. The Spanish settlements which shaped and populated southern California never reached as far north as Humboldt county. Originally a supply center for the Klamath and Trinity gold mines, Eureka was eventually settled by lumbermen seeking the gold to be made in the harvesting of the immense redwoods.

For decades, the city of Eureka was only four blocks wide, bordered on one side by a harbor on the Pacific Ocean and immense virgin forest on the other. To the lumbermen who began to harvest these giants, any talk of sustained yields must have sounded like arguments about draining the ocean, one teaspoon at a time.

After factoring in the discovery of a steam run machine, a steam donkey, which could move the huge logs from the wilderness to the boats, and the demand for lumber after the San Francisco disasters of 1906, and the post War World I and II building booms, the city of Eureka had a guaranteed if somewhat single minded reason to exist. But the mountainous terrain discouraged the building of roads or railways through the area for some time, so the transport of logs remained a job for seamen.

As lumbering and shipbuilding were undertaken mainly by settlers from New England, and because Eureka remained isolation from other influences for so long, the construction and architectural styles of the city began to resemble New England towns. The first buildings were constructed in the Greek Revival style, the predominant architectural style of America at the time. However, as travel and communication improved, new ideas about building methods and styles reached Eureka and the face of the town began to change.

In 1884, two architects from San Francisco, brothers Samuel and Joseph Newsom, came to Eureka with a contract to build a mansion for the region's lumber baron, William Carson. The Newsoms set up a branch office in Eureka and within weeks had drawn up plans for several other buildings in town. William Carson himself employed the brothers to design other buildings as well, including one for his son. A pattern book published by the Newsom brothers influenced local building and design even after they left Eureka to take part in the southern California building boom.

In the 1890's, a pattern book of household furnishings by English designer Charles Eastlake heavily influenced the architectural design of many Eureka homes. The woodworkers in the area were drawn to the decorative shingles, precise detail and turned columns of Eastlake's Victorian styles. This style captured the imagination of the builders, and the influx of residents who came to work for the booming lumber industry gave them many opportunities to use the new style.

Despite a nationwide depression in 1893, Eureka continued to prosper and grow. Between 1880 and 1900, the town's population swelled from 2,600 to well over 7,000. During 1886 and 1887 alone, 257 structures were built in Eureka. Because of the town's continued isolation, very few transients came to Eureka. Most people arrived with a specific objective in mind and stayed. And because the Dolbeer and Carson Lumber Company treated their employees so well, many stayed with the county's largest employer for decades.

The number of imposing Victorian structures built around the turn of century are a tribute to the area's prosperity. Perhaps many of them remain because the owners took such great pride in them. Newspaper articles of the time regularly covered the building of each new addition to the community. And with such a stable population, many of these homes were kept in families for generations.

After the turn of the century, the smaller logging operations in Humboldt county were consolidated by the few largest ones, to better withstand economic fluctuations. In 1914, the railroad came to the county. And with the onset of World War I, the government built shipyards on Humboldt Bay. Eureka did not see again the boom that it enjoyed in the late 1800's, but instead settled into a pattern of slow, but steady, growth.

The Carson mansion stayed in the family until 1950, when the house was purchased by a private businessmen's association, the Ingomar Club. The club has dedicated itself to preserving the mansion as an important part of Eureka's cultural heritage.

In 1972, the restoration of "Old Town" began. Many of the town's best shops and offices are located in restored buildings downtown. These buildings also house numerous galleries and private residences.

In 1973, the Eureka Heritage Society was formed to help restore and maintain the town's many fine old buildings. They have published an architectural history book which describes the details and history of many of the homes in the area. The society is also near completion on a project to have the entire town placed on the registry of historical places.

Traditional Healing Herbs

Up until a hundred years ago, the herbalist was a highly trusted medical professional, who may have spent a lifetime learning the craft. In today's world, herbs are not always viewed by the medical profession as useful therapy, even though many modern drugs are extracted from the same herbs used by herbalists. We would not recommend an herb as a substitute for a doctor's care, but for minor ailments, herbs can be a useful at home treatment. And because herbs are still in food form, they are gentler, easier for the body to process, and less likely to be dependency producing than their over-the-counter counterparts. Here are a few herbs and their uses.

Aloe, or **aloe vera**, is found in many skin treatment preparations. It is a soothing treatment for minor burns and skin inflammations.

Cayenne was used for centuries as an improver of circulation. It was used in the treatment of congestion, sore throats, and colds.

Chamomile is used today mainly as a tea and is known as a mild relaxant and sedative. It should be brewed covered to prevent loss of potency. Brew chamomile tea for treatment of insomnia, menstrual cramps, heartburn, and colic.

Eucalyptus is used in many over-the-counter cold preparations. It can be added to a sauna or steam bath for respiratory ailments. Just placing a branch in a vase in the bath gives a little lift.

Garlic is regaining its reputation as a blood purifier. Recent studies shows it lowers cholesterol, reduces the clotting tendency of blood, and helps lower high blood pressure.

Ginseng has been known as a longevity herb in the Orient for centuries. It is said to produce vigor, especially in men.

Ginger is a diuretic and is given for suppressed menstruation.

Peppermint helps relieve indigestion, heartburn, and nausea. Brew pure tea in a covered container to maintain mint's healing strength.

Raspberry tea is a natural treatment for morning sickness.

Valerian root is the herb from which valium is taken, and should be treated with the same respect. A natural relaxant, valerian root can cause drowsiness and slow down mental functioning.

Two of the most heartening changes taking place in the food industry these days are the shift to local food providers and the increasing commonness of restaurant and inn owned gardens. Some of the local goods purveyors used by the Carters are described in the next chapter. For now, we will discuss gardening in general and the Carter House garden in particular.

Because one of the trademarks of a good restaurant these days is freshness, many in the food service industry have begun growing their own produce. No matter how much care is made in transporting food from the growing site to the processing plant to the preparation site, there is nothing sweeter tasting nor better looking than produce that has been picked that day. By growing their own produce, restaurants ensure themselves that kind of freshness. Even the tiniest of restaurants or inns can benefit from homegrown lettuce and tomatoes.

But restaurants have another reason for "growing their own," the desire to be chemical-free. With more and more information coming to the forefront about food sensitivities and environmental concerns, chefs have become increasingly aware that food needs to do more than just look and taste good. It should also be good for both the people enjoying it and the earth that is providing it. Gardening is a direct way to improve your health and make a small contribution to the environment. Raising vegetables and fruits saves energy and resources used to transport food from distant agricultural regions. And because food raised locally is fresh, it is higher in nutrients than food transported over long distances.

Across the country, restaurants and inns with gardens in the back are becoming commonplace. And because the people growing the food are also the ones cooking and serving it, the word organic is becoming the rule.

Organic gardens are no more difficult to grow than nonorganic ones. They just require a change in awareness, a few new pieces of information, and a little more planning. By planting certain plants next to one another (companion planting), such as a few dill plants among our tomatoes, we can naturally eliminate many of the pests in the garden. And by introducing a few friendly critters, such as earthworms and ladybugs, setting a few lures for other pests, and learning about natural fertilizers, an organic garden can be as bountiful and pest free as its chemical counterpart.

An organic garden begins with good planning. This means choosing a site with good drainage. Soil testing is important, as well as designing the garden so that plants growing together help one another with pest control and nutrient disbursement. Keeping a close eye on the garden's progress is a must.

Compost is an excellent natural fertilizer and aids in any family's or business's recycling program. By feeding the soil, keeping the garden clean and practicing disease prevention, many situations can be resolved before they become problems. Many pests can also be managed with germ warfare, using disease organisms to destroy unwanted intruders.

In most areas, there are companies who specialize in providing organic gardening information and supplies. Several mail order companies which specialize in organic supplies have been established as well. Most libraries have many books on the subject.

Another benefit for restaurants and inns which have their own gardens is the beauty and pleasure these gardens provide the guests. At Carter House, the garden is filled with greens, vegetables, herbs, and flowers. The sweet scents that drift from the garden in the early morning and late afternoon provide a luscious tranquility. There are even a few intentional weeds in the garden, such as chickweed, nettles and sweet cicely. These are there to help the other plants and also because they are themselves tasty. The Hotel Carter serves a "Wild Field Salad" that is a spectacular array of weeds and flowers, all healthful and delicious.

The list of plants to be found in the Carters's gardens is extensive. There are 21 kinds of greens, all picked as babies for extra sweetness and tenderness. The vegetables grown range from beans to squash, from peppers to tomatoes. And because Christi uses herbs and flowers so freely for garnish, the garden is alive with the scents and colors of no less than 30 of these plants.

Gardening is a healthful, relaxing pursuit that provides us with food, exercise, and beauty. Organic gardening has extra health and environmental benefits. By practicing organic gardening at home, we provide ourselves with inexpensive, chemical-free produce. By asking the restaurants and inns where we dine if they grow any of their own foods, we let them know we care about the quality of our food and our planet.

A shady wall can be a
good spot for some
flowering species. The
following flowers thrive
in shady places and will
root well upon a wall:
primrose, kenilworth
ivy, bellflower, and
crested iris.

Fresh Duck Sausage with Polenta and Wild Blackberry Sauce

This appetizer is a culinary tour de force in itself. It is fresh, distinctive, and presents an enormous range of tastes which, together, work sheer magic.

duck sausage, 1 per person
whole chives, for garnish
edible flowers, for garnish

for polenta:
1 cup coarse corn meal
3 1/2 cups water
1 Tablespoon salt
1 clove garlic, crushed
2 cloves shallots, crushed
1 Tablespoon fresh parsley, chopped
1 Tablespoon fresh chives, chopped

for Wild Blackberry Sauce:
3/4 cup red wine
2 Tablespoons crushed shallots
2 cups fresh wild blackberries
2 Tablespoons Tamari
4 Tablespoons + 1 teaspoon garlic, crushed
juice of 2 lemons
4 Tablespoons sugar
1/2 teaspoon white pepper
salt, to taste
additional sugar, to taste

- Salt the water and bring to a boil. Slowly add the cornmeal in a constant stream to prevent lumps from forming. Simmer, stirring constantly, until mixture is very thick and creamy and pulls away from the sides of the pan, about 15 minutes. Remove from heat.

- Add the garlic, shallots, parsley, and chives. Mix well.
- Pour the mixture into a 9 inch tart pan with a removable bottom. Let cool.
- Place the wine, shallots, and 1 teaspoon of the crushed garlic into a saucepan. Reduce over high heat until the wine is virtually gone, approximately 1 Tablespoon of liquid left.
- Place reduced sauce into a food processor and blend with blackberries, Tamari, the remaining garlic, lemon juice, sugar, and white pepper. Add salt and additional sugar to taste.
- Process until very fine, 3 to 5 minutes, and strain through a fine mesh. Set aside in a warm place.
- Split the duck sausage length-wise down the middle, not quite cutting all the way through. Place the sausage open on the grill, with the cut edges down flat. Grill the sausage for about 3 minutes per side.
- Cut polenta into pie shaped wedges, 3 inches across at the wide end. Brush the grill with olive oil. Grill the polenta wedges briefly on both sides until just golden brown.
- Cover bottom of a serving plate with the blackberry sauce. Place duck sausage in the sauce on the plate. Add 1 slice of polenta alongside. Garnish with fresh whole chives and flowers. Serve.

Birds are labeled according to their age, which determines tenderness. Young turkeys may be labeled young turkey, fryer-roaster, young hen, young tom. Young ducks may be labeled duckling, young duckling, broiler duckling, fryer, roast duckling. Young chickens may be labeled young chicken, broiler, fryer, roaster, capon. Mature, less tender birds also have a variety of labels. Chickens may be labeled mature chicken, hen, stewing chicken, fowl. Turkeys can be labeled mature turkey, yearling turkey. Ducks, geese, and guineas may be labeled mature or old. Chicken, turkey, duck, goose, and guineas are also graded. Grade A birds are fully fleshed, meaty, and attractive in appearance. Grade B is less meaty and attractive.

VEGETABLE PLANE

Four primary species of oyster are sold in this country: Pacific, Eastern, Olympia, and European Flat. Pacific oysters are the commonest in the west and have a full briny flavor. Their shells are deeply ridged and may be deeply black, purple, green, or gray. The flesh is usually gray-white to tan. Eastern oysters have a mild flavor. Their tan colored, flat shells may be oblong to round. Meat is usually gray to tan. Olympia oysters are the only ones native to the west coast. They are prized for their sweet flavor, metallic after-taste and tiny greenish shells. Meat ranges from tan to copper-purple. European Flat oysters have a mild, slightly sweet, metallic flavor. Their shells are round and flat and may be white, tan, or greenish. The flesh is usually tan.

Fresh Baked Oysters with Spinach and Fresh Herbs

12 very fresh oysters
2 bunches of spinach, cleaned, chopped, and drained
3 cloves garlic, minced
1 cup bread crumbs
1 cup Parmesan cheese, grated
2 cups rock salt
1/2 cup fresh basil, chopped
1 Tablespoon fresh thyme, chopped
1/4 cup fresh parsley, chopped
1 yellow onion, chopped
1 cube unsalted butter
salt and pepper, to taste

- Place oysters on a baking sheet in a 350° oven until they just begin to open. Shuck the oysters, leaving them in the half shell.
- Sauté the onion and garlic in butter until translucent. Add basil, thyme, and parsley. Sauté lightly.
- Squeeze all excess moisture from the spinach and add to the sauté mixture briefly.
- Remove from the heat and place mixture into a food processor. Process until evenly minced. Do not purée.
- Empty the mixture into a bowl. Stir in the bread crumbs and add salt and pepper.
- Spread rock salt on a baking sheet and place oysters on top. Cover each oyster with a dollop of spinach mixture and a sprinkle of grated Parmesan. Bake at 350° for 15 to 20 minutes. Serve.

Chevre and Prosciutto Biscuit with Orange Rosemary Sauce

for Orange Rosemary Sauce:
2 cups freshly squeezed orange juice
1/4 cup fresh rosemary leaves
1/2 cube unsalted butter

for biscuits:
1/4 pound fresh chevre
2 Tablespoons fresh chives, chopped
1 Tablespoon fresh parsley, chopped
6 fresh homemade biscuits
18 slices of paper-thin Prosciutto

- Place orange juice and rosemary leaves into a saucepan. Over high heat, reduce mixture in volume to a thick, 3/4 cup remnant. Strain out rosemary leaves. Let sauce cool to a lukewarm temperature.
- Slowly add 1/2 cube of cold unsalted butter in small chunks. Whip sauce until all butter is melted. Set sauce aside in a warm place.
- Whip together chevre, chives, and parsley. Set aside.
- Place three layers of very thinly sliced prosciutto on top of each biscuit. On top of prosciutto, add 2 Tablespoons of goat cheese/herb mixture.
- Pour warm Orange Rosemary Sauce over Chevre Prosciutto Biscuit and garnish with fresh rosemary.

A valuable liquid fertilizer is organic, manure tea. Suspend a cloth bag of manure, like a tea bag, into a water filled, air tight container such as a garbage can or 55 gallon drum. Any type of manure will do, the ratio is one part manure to three parts of water. Brew for 24 hours, then remove the manure and dilute the liquid to a pale tea color. Water your plants first with plain water then pour the tea on the soil around the plants. To prevent burning the leaves, do not pour manure tea directly onto the plants.

Grilled Marinated Fresh Prawns

2 pounds unshelled prawns
1/2 cup extra virgin olive oil
1 Tablespoon fresh thyme, chopped
1 Tablespoon fresh rosemary, chopped
1 Tablespoon fresh cilantro, chopped
1 Tablespoon garlic, minced
juice of 1 fresh lime
salt and white pepper, to taste

- Place the prawns in a large bowl. Add olive oil, salt and pepper, fresh herbs, garlic, and lime juice. Marinate well, at least two hours.
- Grill or barbecue the prawns until their shells are a nice pink color. Be careful not to overcook. Serve.

Shrimp are crustaceans with ten legs, but generally the legs and heads have been removed before they are brought to market. There are many different kinds of shrimp, from large to small, and the color of the uncooked shells varies considerably. Related species are langoustines, prawns, and scampi. All of the related species are larger, although there is much disagreement about which name belongs to which. All recipes for one, however, will work for the others.

Smoked Salmon Medallions with Lemon Cream Sauce

quality smoked salmon, moist, room temperature
fresh chives, chopped

for Lemon Cream Sauce:
2 Tablespoons fresh scallions, finely chopped (white parts only)
3 Tablespoons fresh squeezed lemon juice
1 cup fresh butter
1 cup heavy cream
5 Tablespoons water
salt and white pepper, to taste

- Place the scallion, lemon juice and water into a small sauté pan over medium high heat. Add salt and pepper to taste and reduce until only about 2 teaspoons of liquid remain.
- In the meantime, melt the butter over simmering water in the top part of a double boiler.
- When the butter is thoroughly liquefied, strain in the reduced liquid from the sauté pan. Slowly stir in the cream until the sauce is hot and entirely blended. Season with salt and pepper.
- Artfully drizzle the sauce onto individual serving plates. Separate the smoked salmon into nice sized chunks (medallions), and place them onto the plates. Pour a little more sauce on top of the salmon and sprinkle with fresh, chopped chives.
- Serve immediately.

Aquaculture has made a reliable supply of fresh salmon available every month of the year. Some gourmets claim the farmed salmon has a milder flavor and a softer texture than the wilder fish. The color of the flesh also varies according to species and what the fish eat. But wild and farmed species can be used interchangeably.

After a good dinner, one can forgive anybody, even one's own relatives.
. . . Oscar Wilde

Smoked Salmon and Chevre Purses with Mustard Wine Sauce

Many nutritionists recommend that fish be eaten two or more times a week. Fish is very low in cholesterol, is an easily digested food, and is high in protein. Fish is always tender and is cooked to develop flavor.

for Mustard Wine Sauce:
1/4 cup white wine
1/4 cup tarragon vinegar
1/4 cup Dijon mustard
2 cups heavy cream
2 cloves garlic, crushed
2 dashes white pepper
1 dash cayenne pepper
4 scallions, finely chopped
salt, to taste

for salmon:
1 cup smoked salmon
12 long chive strands
12 large Chinese cabbage leaves, 6 inch X 3 inch
1 cup fresh chevre
1 teaspoon lemon juice
1 teaspoon fresh dill
1 teaspoon fresh chives, chopped
1 teaspoon fresh parsley, chopped
1 teaspoon fresh thyme, chopped
salt and pepper, to taste

- Place wine, vinegar, scallions and garlic into a saucepan and reduce until approximately 2 Tablespoons of liquid remain.
- Add cream and reduce over medium heat until sauce is quite thick.
- Add mustard and peppers. Mix thoroughly.
- Strain through a fine mesh. Salt to taste. Set aside in a warm place.
- Very briefly, just a few seconds, blanch the chives and set aside to dry.
- In similar fashion, blanch the cabbage leaves and dry.

> The greatest discovery of my generation is that a human being can alter his life by altering his attitude.
> ... William James

- Whip chevre, lemon juice, dill, chives, parsley, thyme, and salt and pepper together. Fold into the smoked salmon.
- To assemble, place a dollop of chevre/salmon mixture in the center of a cabbage leaf. Fold the edges of the leaf around filling. Tie with a strand of chive. Serve, with sauce on the side, at room temperature.

Here is a way to keep moisture in your garden and weeds out. Put paper feed sacks, any untreated seed sacks, or newspaper between the rows. Weigh them down with hay, manure, or grass clippings. The paper will decompose by the next year's season.

Buy only as much smoked fish as you will use in three days. Refrigerate it immediately, but always bring it to room temperature before serving so that the rich fats can soften and the flavor can be at its best. Because smoked fish is very rich, a little goes a long way.

- Christi

Saffron is made from the dried stigmas of the flowers of the saffron crocus. An enormous number of plants is needed to produce a single pound of the spice, so the cost is always high. Its cultivation and use in the East goes back to antiquity. A pinch of ground saffron will serve to flavor and color a dish. Saffron has a mildly aromatic flavor with a slight aftertaste of iodine. It is an aquired taste.

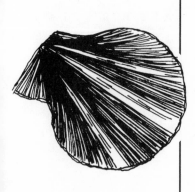

Handmade Salmon / Scallop Ravioli with Cognac Saffron Cream

for ravioli pasta:
2 cups flour
1 teaspoon salt
4 egg yolks
1 Tablespoon extra virgin olive oil
3 Tablespoons water

for Cognac Saffron Cream:
3 cloves shallots
3 Tablespoons Cognac
a very tiny pinch saffron
1/4 cup chicken stock
1 teaspoon fresh garlic, minced
1 teaspoon fresh thyme, minced
1 teaspoon fresh dill, minced
1 teaspoon fresh lemon juice
1 Tablespoon heavy cream
salt and pepper, to taste

for seafood ravioli filling:
1/2 pound fresh salmon, broken up
1/2 pound fresh scallops
3 Tablespoons sweet butter
3 Tablespoons fresh parsley
2 Tablespoons fresh dill
2 Tablespoons fresh chives
fresh squeezed lemon juice
salt and pepper, to taste

- Place flour, salt, egg yolks, olive oil, and water into a processor. Process until the dough is smooth and forms a ball. Add more water if mixture becomes too dry. Wrap dough in plastic and refrigerate for 1 hour.
- Roast shallots under a broiler, turning frequently, until the skins darken.

Heat Cognac and saffron.

- Remove the shallots and purée in a food processor with the other sauce ingredients, including Cognac and saffron mixture.
- Strain mixture through a fine mesh. Set aside.
- Sauté seafood with a small amount of lemon juice in butter, seasoning to taste with salt and pepper. Let cooked salmon/scallop mixture cool.
- Place the seafood in a food processor with parsley, dill, and chives. Process until the mixture constitutes a chunky paste.
- Take cold pasta dough and cut into 2 equal pieces. Preferably using a pasta machine, roll out the first chunk of dough into a long strip, as thin as possible.
- Place 1/2 teaspoon mounds of seafood filling 1 inch apart along the rolled out pasta. Moisten exposed areas around filling mounds with water using a wet pastry brush.
- Roll out the remaining pasta dough to the same shape and thickness as the first. Gently place the second sheet of pasta over the first.
- With the flat side of the thumb, press the two sheets of dough together, working around the mounds of seafood.
- Cut out the ravioli with an appropriately sized cookie cutter or a sharp knife. Place the completed ravioli onto a kitchen towel and prepare to cook. If the ravioli will not be cooked promptly, cover them with another towel until ready to cook.
- Bring salted water to a boil in a large pot. Place ravioli into the boiling water and cook for about 3 minutes. Remove the pasta with a slotted spoon and drain on paper towels.
- Place ravioli onto plates and pour Cognac Saffron Cream over them. Garnish with a variety of chopped fresh herbs.

Cognac is considered, by some connoisseurs, to be one of the three best brandies from France. The other two are Armagnac and Calvados. Cognac is distilled twice, is rich amber in color, and has a smooth flavor. By law it is produced only from Folle Blanche, Colombard, and Saint-Emilion grapes. Armagnac is also a grape brandy, but Calvados is made from apples.

If you look like your passport photo, in all probability you need the journey.
... Earl Wilson

Black Bean and Pumpkin Soup

Actually a duet of two stylish bisques, each soup is excellent on its own. I have described how to make them separately, but at the bottom of the two recipes, I tell you how to combine them for a stunning effect.

Black Bean Soup

1 pound black turtle beans
1 onion, peeled and chopped
1 carrot, peeled and chopped
1 stalk celery, peeled and chopped
6 cloves garlic, chopped
2 Tablespoons fresh cilantro
2 Tablespoons fresh thyme
2 Tablespoons fresh parsley
2 Tablespoons whole pepper corns
1 large ham bone or 1 cup ham scraps
2 to 3 quarts good chicken stock
1 Tablespoon chili powder
1 Tablespoon ground cumin
4 Tablespoons unsweetened cocoa

- Soak the beans overnight in water. Drain.
- In a large, heavy soup pot, combine beans, onion, carrot, celery, garlic, cilantro, thyme, parsley, pepper corns, ham bone (or ham scraps), and 2 to 3 quarts of chicken stock. Cover and bring to a boil.
- Skim off the excess fat, then simmer slowly, loosely covered, until the beans are tender, about 2 hours. Add more chicken stock if necessary to keep the liquid level as high as the beans. Stir often to ensure that the beans cook evenly and do not burn.
- When the bean mixture has been adequately cooked, place it into a processor to purée. After the bean mixture is fully puréed, place it back into the soup pot and blend in the

A bisque is a rich, creamy soup which often contains shellfish.

WIRE SPOON FOR BESTING SAUCES

A heavy meal begins best with an unthickened stock soup; a light meal is best started with a soup of the cream variety.

— Christi

cumin, chili powder, and cocoa. Keep warm.

Pumpkin Soup

1 large fresh pumpkin
1 large onion
4 cloves garlic, chopped
1 carrot, chopped
1 celery stalk, chopped
3/4 cup white wine
3/4 cup champagne vinegar
4 cups heavy cream
salt and pepper, to taste

- Remove seed and pulp and cut the pumpkin into good size pieces. Place the pumpkin in a pan with 1/2 inch of water in the bottom. Cover pan with foil and bake pumpkin in a 350° oven until the meat becomes very, very soft, about 1 hour.
- Purée the pumpkin meat very well, approximately 5 minutes in a food processor.
- In a separate pan, mix onion, garlic, carrot, celery stalk, white wine, and champagne vinegar. Reduce over high heat until there are just a few Tablespoons of liquid left.
- Add the 4 cups cream. Reduce sauce over lower heat to approximately 3 cups in volume - creamy, but not too thick. Mix in pumpkin purée and salt and pepper to taste.

To serve the two soups together:

Take 1 ladle of the pumpkin soup and 1 ladle of the black bean soup and pour them slowly and simultaneously into opposite sides of an individual size bowl. The dark and light soup should remain separate, filling the soup bowl evenly and forming a line down the center of the bowl. Garnish the soups with crème fraîche, a sprig of cilantro, and a touch of salsa.

The pumpkin soup recipe also works well with butternut squash.
- Christi

In the United States, over 90% of all pumpkins sold are for decoration.

Fresh Corn / Butternut Squash Soup with Roasted Red Pepper Cream

Crème fraîche:

1 cup heavy cream
2 Tablespoons
   buttermilk

Bring cream and buttermilk to room temperature. Combine in a warmed glass jar. Cover the jar securely, and set in a warm place (approximately 75°). Allow mixture to thicken for 8 hours or more. Refrigerate after crème fraîche thickens appropriately. Crème fraîche will keep in the refrigerator for 10 days. Yields 1 cup.

for Corn Butternut Squash Soup:
2 large fresh butternut squash
4 to 5 fresh ears of corn, kernels removed from cob
1 large onion
4 cloves garlic, chopped
1 carrot, chopped
1 celery stalk, chopped
3/4 cup white wine
3/4 cup champagne vinegar
4 cups heavy cream
salt and pepper, to taste
fresh cilantro for garnish

for Roasted Red Pepper Cream:
4 red bell peppers
3 cloves shallots
1 teaspoon fresh garlic, minced
1 teaspoon fresh thyme, minced
1 teaspoon fresh dill, minced
1 teaspoon fresh lemon juice
1 Tablespoon heavy cream
salt and pepper, to taste

- Place squash in a pan with 1/2 inch of water in bottom. Cover pan with foil and bake squash in a 350° oven until they become very very soft, about 1 hour.
- Roast peppers and shallots under broiler, turning frequently, until the pepper skins darken significantly.
- Remove the shallots and peppers from broiler. Place peppers into a paper sack. Clo sack tightly and let it sit for approximately 30 minutes to allow the pepper skins to loosen.
- Peel peppers and purée in a food processo

A dog is a dog except when he is facing you. Then he is Mr. Dog.
... Haitian farmer

with shallots, garlic, thyme, dill, lemon juice, cream, salt, and pepper. Strain mixture through a fine mesh. Set the sauce aside in a warm place.

- Remove squash from oven and let cool. Purée squash very well, about 5 minutes in a food processor. Mix in the corn.
- In a separate pan, mix onion, garlic, carrot, celery, white wine, and champagne vinegar. Reduce over high heat until there are just a few Tablespoons of liquid left in the pan.
- Add cream. Reduce sauce over lower heat to approximately 3 cups in volume - creamy, but not too thick.
- Mix in the squash purée and corn. Salt and pepper to taste.
- To serve, place soup in bowls. Drizzle Red Pepper Cream over the soup in an eye pleasing pattern. Place a dollop of crème fraîche onto the soup. Garnish with a sprig of fresh cilantro.

Experts say there are over 1000 varieties of peppers. We have taken the name chile from Mexico, pimento from the Spanish, and the word pepper is English. Confusion abounds. Here are a few of the common peppers used in cooking.

Sweet Peppers - include the familar bell peppers and Italian peppers. Available year around.

Serrano - are colored red or green and are very hot. Used extensively by Mexican cooks, but can be cooled by removing the ribs and seeds.

Cayenne - are usually dried and ground.

Jalapeño - plump little chiles with green skins. Hot, but manageable and the most available of all the green chiles.

Banana pepper - range in taste from mild to medium hot. These chiles are long tapering cones with a creamy yellow skin. They are often pickled.

Pablano (ancho) - Shiny skins colored red or green. Medium heat but deep flavor.

Anaheim - elongated with a light twist. Red or green and mild to medium hot.

Beet Bisque
with Chive Crème Fraîche

2 to 3 pounds beets
2 onions
3 garlic cloves, crushed
salt and pepper, to taste
1/2 cup heavy cream
chives

- In water, cook the beets until tender. Cool the beets, saving the cooking water.
- Sauté onion and garlic together. Purée and set aside.
- When the beets are cool, the skins should come off easily. Remove the beet skins and purée them.
- Add the beets, onions, and garlic and purée. Thin the mixture with the water used for cooking the beets. Add the cream.
- Strain, then salt and pepper to taste. To serve top with Chive Crème Fraîche and chopped chives.

Chive Crème Fraîche:

1 cup heavy cream
2 Tablespoons
    buttermilk
2 Tablespoons chives,
    finely chopped

Bring cream and buttermilk to room temperature, then combine with chives in a warmed glass jar. Cover securely and let sit at room temperature (approximately 75°) for 8 hours or until desired thickness is achieved. Store in the refrigerator for up to 10 days.
Yield 1 cup.

Fresh Yellow Squash and Tomato Bisque

yellow squash, a pound or more (depending on the
    amount of soup you want to make)
tomatoes, same amount as the squash
1 anaheim pepper, chopped
1 clove garlic, chopped
1/2 cup onions, chopped
1/3 cup white wine
2 Tablespoons olive oil
Tamari, to taste
Worcestershire sauce, to taste
salt and pepper, to taste
1/2 cup heavy cream

- Slice squash. Chop tomatoes. Set aside.
- Sauté the onions and pepper in olive oil until softened. Add garlic, squash, and tomatoes. Cook for a minute or so.
- Add white wine, cover, and simmer until squash begins to soften. Remove from heat.
- In a processor, purée the above. Add salt and pepper, Tamari, and Worcestershire to taste. Mix very well.
- Strain. Add the cream. Blend well and adjust the seasoning if desired.

For many years people would not eat tomatoes for fear of being poisoned. The tomato is a member of the deadly nightshade family. After discovering a person wouldn't die after eating a tomato, word got around that tomatoes caused insanity. Now it is one of our most popular vegetables. They don't freeze well, but they do can well so they are available throughout the year.

When cooking tomatoes you might consider adding one teaspoon of sugar for every 4 or 5 tomatoes. It does not make them sweet, but it does bring out their color and flavor.

- Christi

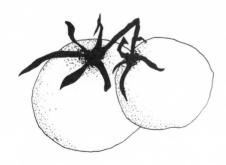

Spinach and Carrot Cream Soup

Like the black bean and squash soups, these two soups can be served together for a delicious and stunning effect. Again, I have provided the separate recipes and how to serve them together.

Spinach Soup

3 1/2 pounds fresh spinach, well washed
1/4 cup unsalted butter
2 cups onions, finely chopped
2 cups chicken stock
2 cups heavy cream
salt and pepper, to taste
assorted fresh herbs, chopped, for garnish

- Place spinach in a large pot. Add enough water to just cover the spinach. Cover and cook on high heat until the leaves are wilted and tender.
- While the spinach is cooking, melt the butter in a large pan, add the onions, and sauté un they are translucent and golden.
- Drain the spinach, reserving the liquid. In a processor, purée the spinach along with the onion until the mixture is smooth.
- Combine the puréed mixture with the chicken stock, the cream, and the liquid in which the spinach was cooked. Slowly bring to a simmer. Add salt and pepper to taste.

Spinach is the basis for dishes called Florentine.

— Christi

Spinach, as well as other vegetables, was once used for coloring homemade cosmetic preparations. Here are a couple of recipes for homemade cosmetics.

Natural Blush

juice of 6 carrots
juice of 1/2 beet
6 ounces cornstarch

Mix all ingredients and spread onto a flat dish. Place in the sun to dry, stirring occasionally.

Carrot Soup

2 1/2 pounds fresh carrots, peeled and ends cut
1/4 cup unsalted butter
1 1/2 cups onions, finely chopped
2 cups chicken stock
2 cups heavy cream
salt and pepper, to taste
assorted herbs, chopped, for garnish

- Place the carrots in a large pot. Just cover them with water. Cover and cook over high heat until the carrots are tender.
- While the carrots are cooking, melt butter in a large pan and sauté the onions until they are translucent and golden.
- Drain the carrots, reserving the liquid. In a processor, purée the carrots along with the onion until the mixture is smooth.
- Combine the puréed mixture with the chicken stock, the cream, and the liquid in which the carrots were cooked. Slowly bring to a simmer. Add salt and pepper to taste.

To serve the two soups together:
Take 1 ladle of the spinach soup and 1 ladle of the carrot soup and pour them slowly and simultaneously into opposite sides of an individual bowl. The soups should remain separate, filling the soup bowl evenly and forming a distinct line down the approximate center of the bowl. Garnish with fresh, finely chopped herbs. Serve.

Homemade Wrinkle Cream

2 Tablespoons cocoa
  butter
2 teaspoons rose water
3 Tablespoons olive oil
1/2 teaspoon honey
2 Tablespoons lanolin

Place cocoa butter, olive oil, and lanolin in a glass dish in a pan of hot water on low heat. Stir with a wooden spoon until smooth. Remove dish from pan and add rose water and honey. Cool and then beat until well blended. Store in a glass jar.

HANDLED CASSEROLE
INDIVIDUAL SIZE

The average American consumes 8 1/2 pounds of carrots per year.

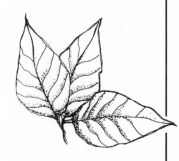

Fresh Pea Soup with Mint Crème Fraîche

6 cups fresh peas, shelled
1/4 cup sweet butter
1/2 cup onion
1 cup fresh leeks, chopped (white parts only)
2 cups heavy cream
1 teaspoon fresh squeezed lemon juice
2 cups chicken stock
salt and pepper, to taste
fresh herbs, your choice, chopped

- In a large sauté pan, melt the butter and sauté the peas, leeks, and onions. Season with salt and pepper.
- Place this mixture into a food processor with the lemon juice. Process until mixture takes on a smooth consistency. With the processor still operating, slowly add the chicken stock and blend well.
- Pour the resulting mixture through a strainer into a large saucepan and warm over low heat. Add the cream and season to taste with salt and pepper. Mix well and gently warm.
- Place the soup in bowls and add a dollop of Mint Crème Fraîche to each serving.

Mint Crème Fraîche

1 cup heavy cream
2 Tablespoons buttermilk
1 Tablespoon fresh mint, chopped

Bring cream and buttermilk to room temperature. Combine cream, buttermilk and mint in a warmed glass jar. Cover the jar securely and set in a warm place, (approximately 75° F.) Allow mixture to thicken for 8 hours or more. Refrigerate after crème fraîche thickens appropriately. Makes approximately 1 cup. Keeps for 10 days refrigerated.

Cream of Asparagus Soup

3 pounds fresh asparagus, tender parts only
1/4 cup sweet butter
1/2 cup onion
1 cup fresh leeks, chopped (white parts only)
2 cups heavy cream
1 teaspoon fresh squeezed lemon juice
2 cups chicken stock
salt and pepper to taste
fresh herbs, your choice, chopped

- In a large sauté pan, melt butter and sauté asparagus, leeks, and onions, seasoning with salt and pepper.
- Place this mixture into a food processor with the lemon juice. Process until the mixture takes on a smooth consistency. With the processor still operating, slowly add the chicken stock and blend well.
- Pour the resulting mixture through a strainer into a large saucepan. Warm over low heat.
- Add the cream, and season to taste with salt and pepper.
- Mix well and gently warm. Sprinkle soup with chopped herbs and serve. Soup may be garnished with crème fraîche or sour cream if desired.

Asparagus is an early spring plant and is a member of the Lily-of-the-Valley family. It is considered a luxury.

In France asparagus is drained and presented on a folded white napkin with an individual bowl of Hollandaise sauce into which it is dipped. Often it is served as a separate course to be savored without distraction.

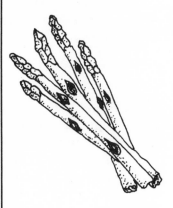

Soaking seeds overnight in a warm dark place speeds germination.

Flowers and Their Seasons

Many gardeners look forward to the first bloom of spring. Yet, there ar plants which bloom in other seasons as well. By planting carefully gardens can have a hint of color year round. Here are the most wide grown color producers and their blooming season. Common names a used where possible.

Spring:

daffodil	white marguerites	columbine	rockcress
aster	basket-of-gold	English daisy	larkspur
sweet william	foxglove	coral bells	candytuft
primrose	pansy	iris	California poppies
snapdragons	marigold	tulips	violet

Summer:

yarrow	columbine	aster	begonia
daisy	periwinkle	Gladiolus	chrysanthemum
Dahlia	foxglove	Gaillardia	bleeding heart
carol bells	Hibiscus	petunia	phlox
Zinnia	verbena	black-eyed susan	

Fall:

Anemone	golden marguereite	African daisy	aster
Begonia	fibrous bellflower	Campanula	foxglove
Delphinium	Hydrangea	goldenrod	Fuchsia
marigold	fairy lily	Camellia	crimson flag
Gaillardia grandiflora			

Winter:

winter blooming bergenia	Kaffir lily	Crocus
winter aconite	Tulbaghia	Acacia
Camellia		

Among the finest restaurants these days, the buzzword is local. We have found that the best places always have a strong commitment to freshness. During the eighties, that sometimes meant flying in fish from Alaska twice a week or express shipping cheesecakes from New York every day.

The nineties have brought new sensibilities. We recognize that there are often people in our communities who provide excellent products; fresh, reasonably priced, the result of regional expertise. Besides the fact that locally grown products are the freshest with the least amount of trouble and that they reflect a regional emphasis, buying locally also supports our communities. We keep dollars in the neighborhood and provide jobs for friends rather than strangers. Further, because local industries are smaller and closely tied to the community, they tend to be more environmentally conscious.

Carter House and Hotel Carter are very conscientious about using local products. They, like the best of many small enterprises, even grow their own vegetables, flowers and, herbs. We talked with John Salizzoni, the hotel dining room manager, about this philosophy. John has worked with the Carters since they opened Carter House. He is a marvelous chef in his own right and has sought out many local entrepreneurs for the products they provide the Carter kitchens.

With the Napa Valley just hours down the road, the hotel has easy access to some of the finest wines in the world. A few of John's favorite selections are listed at the end of the main and side dish section. He also shares what it is he likes about the wines and foods he feels the wines best compliment.

The closest wineries, however, are right in Humboldt County. Arcata boasts three excellent wine makers. Free Run Winery produces

200 cases annually of merlot, riesling, chardonnay, and pinot noir. Oliveira Winery specializes in premium red wines, chenin blanc, and white zinfandel. Fieldbrook Valley Winery produces 1000 cases a year of several varietals, including chardonnay, sauvignon blanc, and cabernet. In southern Humboldt county, we find Briceland Vineyards, producing 1000 cases a year, mostly for local consumption. Willowcreek Vineyards is a family run winery located in McKinleyville.

There are two local breweries. Lost Coast Brewery, in downtown Eureka, is owned by Barbara Groom and Wendy Pound. A restaurant in the front of the building serves excellent food, cajun is a specialty. In the back of the building, plainly visible behind large windows, are the fermentation tanks. There are generally four brews available each day. Humboldt Brewery is located in Arcata and also features food designed to inspire a taste for beer.

Both Carter House and Hotel Carter make excellent use of local seafood, especially salmon, a spring and summer specialty, and crab, which comes into season in December. But the kitchens also utilize Roger Lawson's specialty meats. He smokes the meat in small batches and uses only lean cuts. Most people who have sampled Roger's meats agree his process is superior to the industrialized, mass produced meats found in large markets.

Although the kitchen staff turns out most of their own pastries and breads, the wonderful loaves of sourdough which grace the tables in the hotel dining room are made by Eureka Baking Company. By the way, the idea of having those loaves laid out on the table that way is to encourage the guests to make a mess. Please do not feel the need to be proper, we were told. The best way to eat bread is to break it, then dip it in butter or olive oil. The crumbs are just part of the fun.

Both Carter kitchens use loads of a naturally grown local wonder, chanterelle mushrooms. These mushrooms are hand picked and delivered by an energetic retiree named Ludwig. As he was making a delivery, we stopped him to asked how he came by these luscious beauties. "Nature does much of the work for me," he told us in a heavy German accent. "I only need the eyes to see them and the hand to pick them."

There is a booming cheese industry in Humboldt county. Much of it is the popular chevre, goat cheese. For that reason, you will find many of Christi's recipes contain chevre. She is utilizing a local industry. Among the best known is Mary Konnersman's Cypress Grove cheese, located in McKinleyville, just north of Eureka. Mary believes in keeping her goats happy. Her pampering has paid off as her animals have set national records for milk production. Increasing her production has allowed her to keep up with a growing demand and she now processes 1,000 gallons a week during peak season.

A sweet treat of local origin is Mad River Farms jams, marmalades, and conserves. Owned by Susan Anderson and Chris Ursich, this little company began making jams commercially for use in a friend's bagel shop, Los Bagels. So many customers wanted the jam that they moved into retail sales of their products. They sell their jam mail order as well, packed in a redwood crate, and offer popsicles and cheesecakes at local craft fairs.

These are just a sampling of the wonderful products made in Humboldt county. Every community in the country has local growers, producers, bakers, and artists who promote the best of their region. As more and more cottage industries learn marketing savvy and as more and more grocers and restaurants recognize the value of local products, the food industry is becoming more personal, fresher, and more regionally expressive. This is a change for the better in our book.

Apple / Sausage / Sage Sauté in Phyllo with Brown Garlic Sauce

Phyllo is a pastry made up of multi-layered, very thin sheets of dough. You may also find it spelled filo or fillo.

The dough is ethnic in origin. You have probably enjoyed it in Greek and Middle Eastern dishes. My first recommendation is that you buy the dough at a local ethnic pastry shop. But if that is not possible, excellent dough is available from your grocer's freezer.

-Christi

for Apple / Sausage / Sage Sauté:
3 Granny Smith apples, cored, peeled, and sliced
1/4 cup unsalted butter, melted
4 Tablespoons onions, diced
1 Tablespoon fresh lemon juice
1/2 pound mild Italian sausage
4 Tablespoons fresh sage, chopped
salt and pepper, to taste
4 ounces chevre
phyllo dough, thawed if frozen

for Brown Garlic Sauce:
2 cups cold water
20 cloves garlic, peeled
1 Tablespoon Tamari
1 1/2 cups chicken stock
1 Tablespoon arrowroot
salt and pepper, to taste

for garnishment:
fresh parmesan, grated
fresh sage, chopped
sweet marjoram, chopped
parsley, chopped

- In a sauté pan, sauté onions, apples, and lemon juice in melted butter until the onion and apples caramelized. Set aside.
- In another sauté pan, sauté sausage with sage, salt, and pepper until the meat is done. Set aside.
- Preheat the oven to 400°. Line the bottom of 9 inch tart pan with about 8 layers of phyllo dough, basting between layers with melted butter.
- To construct, place a layer of the apple/onion

mixture onto the phyllo. Next, layer the sausage onto the dough. On top of these layers, place dabs of goat cheese.

- When all the ingredients have been place onto the dough, push the edges of the phyllo toward the center, in effect enclosing the ingredients inside a pouch of phyllo dough, pinching the dough together at the top.
- Place the phyllo pouch on an ungreased cookie sheet and bake in the oven for 30 to 35 minutes or until golden brown.
- Place garlic cloves and water into a sauce pan. Bring water to a boil and simmer for 5 minutes. Drain.
- Add Tamari and chicken stock to the drained garlic and boil for about 10 minutes.
- With a small amount of water, make a paste of the arrowroot and add to the sauce to thicken it. Season the sauce with salt and pepper to taste.
- To serve, pour the Brown Garlic Sauce onto the bottom of the serving plate. Cut the phyllo tart and place slices on the plate. Sprinkle with freshly grated parmesan cheese and fresh chopped sage, sweet marjoram, and parsley.

Serves 4.

Garlic stores best in a cool place where air circulates. The best bags for storage are the net ones that allow air around the cloves. Garlic will not release its odor until peeled or cut.

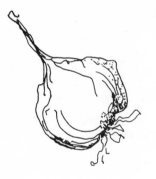

Putting food on a cold plate is like putting a baby down on a marble floor.
... Overheard from a restaurant patron

American bacon can be substituted for pancetta.

Pan Fried River Trout and Pancetta with Cream Sauces

for trout:
6 fresh stream trout, cleaned and whole
1/4 cup pinenuts, roasted
1/2 teaspoon salt
1 onion, chopped
1/2 teaspoon white pepper
1/3 pound pancetta, thick sliced and cut into 1 inch pieces
1/4 cup extra virgin olive oil
1 cup cornmeal

for Lemon Cream Sauce:
2 Tablespoons scallions, finely chopped (white part only)
3 Tablespoons fresh squeezed lemon juice
1 cup butter
1 cup heavy cream
5 Tablespoons water
salt and white pepper, to taste

for Cilantro Cream Sauce:
2 Tablespoons scallions, finely chopped (white parts only)
3 Tablespoons fresh squeezed lime juice
1 cup butter
1 cup heavy cream
5 Tablespoons water
1/2 cup fresh cilantro, finely chopped
salt and white pepper, to taste

- Begin with the Lemon Cream Sauce. Place the scallions, lemon juice, and water into a small sauté pan over medium high heat. Add a little salt and pepper to taste and reduce until only about 2 teaspoons of liquid remain.
- In the meantime, melt the butter over simmering water in the top part of a double

boiler. When butter is thoroughly liquefied, strain in the reduced liquid from the sauté pan. Slowly stir in the cream until the sauce is hot and entirely blended.

- Season with salt and pepper and set aside in a warm place.
- To make the Cilantro Cream Sauce, place the scallions, lime juice, and water into a small sauté pan over medium high heat. Add a little salt and pepper to taste and reduce until about 2 teaspoons of liquid remain.
- In the meantime, melt the butter over simmering water in the top part of a double boiler. When butter is thoroughly liquefied, strain in the reduced liquid from the sauté pan. Slowly stir in the cream and cilantro until the sauce is hot and entirely blended.
- Season with salt and pepper and set aside in a warm place.
- Rinse the trout under cold water and leave them wet. Season the fish with salt and pepper, especially the insides.
- Place the cornmeal on a large dish and coat the trout with the cornmeal.
- In a large heavy skillet, heat the olive oil over medium high heat and add the pancetta. Sauté the pancetta until it is almost, but not quite, cooked, about 3 minutes.
- Leaving the fat in the skillet, remove the pancetta and drain on towels. Place the trout into the skillet. Do not crowd or stack them.
- Fry the trout on one side for 4 minutes, or until the bottom is golden brown. Flip the fish and cook for about 5 minutes on the second side.
- Gently remove the trout from the skillet and let drain on paper towels. Drain most the fat from the skillet, but not all, and return the pancetta to the skillet with the onion. Cook

Here is one more reason not to bring those plastic storage bags home from the grocer. Lettuce and celery will stay crisp longer if you store them in the refrigerator in paper bags, instead of plastic.

A few gardening terms:
Annual - a plant that completes its growth cycle in one year.
Biennial - a plant that takes two years to complete its growth cycle.
Bolting - going to seed, generally because conditions are too warm for the plant. When a vegetable plant shoots up a seed stalk, its edible leaves become bitter.
Broadcast - scatter seeds uniformly rather than plant in rows or patterns.
Cold frame - a seed starter consisting of a bottomless box with a glass lid. It protects plants from the elements.
Compost - plant and other organic matter mixed and piled together in a manner which encourages decay and decomposition and then later used for fertilizing and conditioning land.
Growth cycle - from seed to flower to fruit to seed.
Hotbed - a bottomless box like a cold frame,

over medium heat for about 1 minute, or until the onion softens adequately.
- Add pinenuts and sauté mixture briefly to thoroughly heat the pinenuts.
- Drizzle individual warmed plates with Lemon Cream Sauce. Place the trout over the sauce on the plates. Top the trout with the pinenuts/pancetta mixture and cover with Cilantro Cream Sauce. Serve immediately.

Serves 6.

Classic Fresh Crab

fresh crab
bay leaves, 1 for each crab
1 Tablespoon salt
drawn butter
fresh lemon

- In a large kettle, bring water to a rolling boil. Add a bay leaf for each crab to be cooked and 1 Tablespoon salt to the boiling water.
- Place as many live crabs into the boiling water as will easily fit into the kettle. Boil crabs for 25 minutes.
- Remove crabs from the boiling water and rinse under cold water until they are cool. Remove backs, gills, and innards. Crack crabs and serve with drawn butter and lemon.

but with additional heating from an electrical source or from decomposing manure. Used like a cold frame to protect and start plants.
Hybrid - a plant derived from a cross pollination of different species.
Mule - an infertile hybrid.
NPK - the three major nutrients: nitrogen (n), phosphorus (p), and potassium (k).
Perennial - a plant with a growth cycle lasting longer than two years.
Raised beds - planted areas in which the growing area, higher than the surrounding walk ways, is more densely planted to facilitate maintenence, to utilize more efficiently the water used, and to gather large harvests from small plots.
Rotation - planting different crops in the same growing area, one after the other, so that the soil is replenished by the succeeding crop and the growing seasons are used to the fullest.

Fresh Crab Roulade with Red Pepper Cream Sauce

for filling:
1 cup fresh crab meat
1 cup cream cheese
1 Tablespoon sour cream
1 teaspoon chives, chopped
1 teaspoon thyme, chopped
1 teaspoon dill, chopped
salt and pepper, to taste

A roulade is a slice of meat or pastry rolled with a filling, usually consisting of minced meat, and cooked.

for roulade:
4 eggs, separated
1/3 cup sugar
1/4 teaspoon cream of tartar
2/3 cup cake flour, sifted

This dish also makes a great appetizer.
- Christi

for Roasted Red Pepper Cream Sauce:
2 red bell peppers
2 cups heavy cream
1/2 cup white wine
2 dashes white pepper
1 dash cayenne pepper
4 scallions, finely chopped
2 cloves garlic, minced
salt, to taste

- Whip cream cheese with sour cream, chives, thyme, and dill. Fold in the crab meat and then add salt and white pepper. Set aside in cool place.
- Preheat oven to 350°. Lightly grease and flour an 11 inch X 15 inch jelly roll pan. Line bottom with parchment paper.
- In a large bowl, beat egg yolks to break them up. Add sugar and continue to beat until the mixture falls from the beater in a ribbon and leaves a slowly dissolving trail on the surface (ribbon stage).

- In a separate large copper or stainless steel bowl, beat egg whites until just foamy. Add cream of tartar. Beat whites until stiff, glossy peaks form.
- Fold flour into the yolk mixture in three stages. Then fold in 1/3 of the whites to lighten. Very gently fold in remaining whites.
- Fill prepared pan with batter and bake until top springs back when gently pressed with finger, about 15 minutes.
- Cool in pan 5 minutes. Turn cake out onto a kitchen towel covered with a sheet of parchment paper. Remove paper from the cake bottom and trim crusts all around. Carefully roll up in the parchment, wrap with a kitchen towel to secure and cool completely on a wire rack.
- Gently unroll, then spread crab filling to within 1 inch of edges. Gently reroll, then refrigerate roulade for 2 hours. Remove from refrigerator and bring to room temperature.
- Roast red peppers until the skins darken. Remove the skins. Purée the peppers in a food processor.
- Place wine, scallions, and garlic into a saucepan and reduce until approximately 2 Tablespoons of wine remain.
- Add cream and reduce over medium heat until mixture thickens. Add salt and peppers.
- Add cream mixture to the purée in the processor and purée completely. Strain through a fine mesh.
- To serve, cover roulade with the pepper sauce. Garnish as desired.

Happiness: a good bank account, a good cook, and a good digestion.

... Jean Jacques Rousseau

Mixed Grill: Mahi Mahi and Alaskan Halibut with Mango / Cilantro / Lime Sauce

A grilled fish is especially dramatic when the fish is served whole. To bone a whole fish, cut into the fish from the top along both sides of the backbone. When the backbone is loosened, cut it off with scissors at the tail and head ends. When you pull it out, be careful to bring out the smaller bones attached to it. The first time you bone a fish, you may find it tough going, but it gets easier each time, as any fisherman will tell you.

- Christi

for Mango / Cilantro / Lime Sauce:
2 mangos, peeled, de-seeded and chopped into chunks
2 to 3 Tablespoons fresh cilantro
salt and pepper, to taste
juice of 1 lime

for Mixed Grill:
fresh Mahi Mahi
fresh Alaskan Halibut
juice of 2 lemons
2 Tablespoons extra virgin olive oil
1 Tablespoon fresh dill, chopped
salt and pepper, to taste

- In a food processor, purée the mango, cilantro, salt, pepper, and lime juice until mixture is smooth and creamy. Transfer the mixture into a saucepan and warm gently.
- Mix lemon juice, dill, salt, pepper, and olive oil together for basting sauce.
- Grill fish until appropriately cooked, basting frequently with basting sauce. Do not overcook.
- To serve, place fish on a warmed plate. Add sauce and garnish.

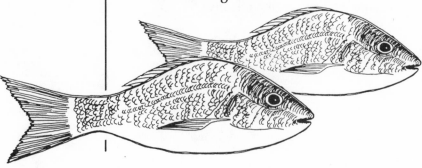

Grilled Snapper with Beurre Blanc Sauce

for Beurre Blanc Sauce:
1/4 cup dry white wine
juice of 1/2 lemon
3 garlic cloves, crushed
1 cup sweet butter
salt and pepper, to taste

for fish:
fresh snapper, 1 piece per person
minced garlic
salt and pepper, to taste
fresh squeezed lemon juice

- Bring wine, lemon juice, and garlic to a boil over medium heat. Boil until liquid reduces down to 1 1/2 Tablespoons in volume. This will happen very rapidly, approximately 3 minutes.
- Reduce heat to very low. Whip in chunks of butter slowly. When all butter is mixed in and melted, salt and pepper to taste. Keep warm.
- Season fish to taste with salt, pepper, lemon, and garlic. Grill until done.
- To serve, place fish on a warmed plate, cover   with sauce and serve.

When grilling fish, rub the grill with olive oil to prevent sticking. If you use butter or margarine, the fish will stick to it.

Cold air, like water, flows down hill. When planning a garden site, avoid choosing a spot in a hollow.

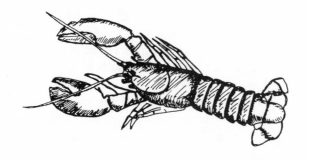

Fresh Salmon Cakes with Spicy Lemon / Mustard Sauce

for salmon cakes:
1/2 red bell pepper, finely diced
1/2 green bell pepper, finely diced
2 garlic cloves, chopped
1 Tablespoon olive oil
2 Tablespoons white wine, or water
1 pound fresh salmon meat
1/2 cup fresh fine white bread crumbs
3 scallions, thinly sliced
3 to 4 Tablespoons heavy cream
salt and pepper, to taste
dash of tabasco sauce
1 to 2 dashes Worcestershire sauce
olive oil, for frying

for Spicy Lemon / Mustard Sauce:
4 garlic cloves, finely chopped
juice of 1 lemon
2 Tablespoons white wine, or water
1 cup heavy cream
1 Tablespoon Dijon mustard
salt and pepper, to taste
tabasco, to taste
Worcestershire sauce, to taste

Pound for pound, fish supplies about as much protein as beef or pork, with only half the calories. At least 240 species of fish are sold in the United States and consumption is at an all time high.

- Sauté peppers and garlic in olive oil. Add white wine and cook until liquid evaporates. Remove from heat.
- Break up salmon meat, but do not chop. Mix salmon with bread crumbs. Mix in sautéed peppers, garlic, and raw scallions.
- Add cream until mixture binds, but is not mushy. Season to taste with salt, pepper, tabasco, and Worcestershire. Cover and refrigerate for at least an hour.
- Fifteen minutes before you are ready to cook salmon, make sauce. Cook garlic, lemon juice

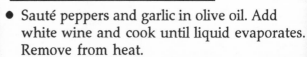

and wine over medium heat until very little liquid is left in the saucepan.
- Add cream and bring to a boil. Reduce heat and simmer about 10 minutes until sauce is thickened.
- Stir in mustard, salt, pepper, a dash of tabasco, and a dash of Worcestershire sauce. Set aside in a warm place.
- Shape salmon mixture into 3 ounce patties and fry in olive oil until golden brown. Drain on paper towels.
- Serve cakes with sauce while still warm.

Makes 8 cakes, serves 4.

Seafood Cuts:
Whole - fish are sold just as they come from the water.
Drawn - fish have been scaled and eviscerated.
Steaks - cross sections, up to an inch thick, taken from a large fish.
Fillets - the flesh is sliced lengthwise, without the bone.
Portions or sticks - pieces cut from frozen blocks of lean, white ocean fish.

Grilled Fresh Salmon with Tri-Colored Salsa

A colorful and unique way to prepare fresh salmon - impressive visually and singularly delicious.

---

for yellow salsa:
1 sweet golden pepper
1 yellow onion
3 cloves garlic
1 jalapeño pepper
6 yellow tomatoes
1 teaspoon fresh lemon juice
1 Tablespoon fresh cilantro
1 Tablespoon fresh parsley
1 teaspoon cumin
1 Tablespoon coarse grain yellow mustard
salt and white pepper, to taste

---

for green salsa:
1 anaheim pepper
1 green bell pepper
2 green onions
1 white onion
2 cloves garlic
1 jalapeño pepper
6 tomatoes
1 teaspoon lime juice
2 Tablespoons cilantro
1 Tablespoon green mustard
salt and white pepper, to taste

---

for red salsa:
1 red onion
1 red sweet pepper
1 cayenne pepper
3 cloves garlic
3 large red tomatoes
1 teaspoon raspberry vinegar
1 teaspoon cumin
1 Tablespoon tomato paste

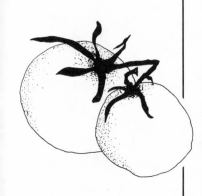

Don't go to sleep.
So many people
die there.
... Mark Twain

salt and white pepper, to taste

---

for salmon:
3 pounds salmon, for fillets, not steaks
extra virgin olive oil
corn husks, for garnish
cayenne pepper, for garnish

- Preheat oven to 350°.
- Chop peppers, garlic, and onion for the yellow salsa into large chunks and mix. Place on a baking sheet.
- Chop peppers, onions, and garlic for the green salsa into chunks and mix. Place on a baking sheet.
- Chop onion, peppers, and garlic for the red salsa in the same manner.
- Place all three baking sheets in the preheated oven and dry roast the chopped mixture for about 45 minutes, or until ingredients are well softened.
- Boil water in a large pot. Score the skins, and place all 15 tomatoes into the boiling water. Boil until their skins begin to peel away. Place in cold water. Once cool, separate the 6 yellow tomatoes, the 6 green salsa tomatoes, and the 3 large red salsa tomatoes.
- Peel, core, and seed tomatoes, keeping them separate, then cut into chunks.
- Mix yellow tomato chunks with yellow salsa roasted ingredients. Add lemon juice, fresh cilantro, parsley, cumin, and mustard. Process mixture briefly, it should remain chunky. Salt and pepper to taste. Set aside.
- Add lime juice, cilantro, green mustard, salt, and white pepper to 6 green salsa tomatoes. Add green salsa roasted ingredients to mixture. Process briefly, then set aside.
- Mix together all red salsa ingredients. Process as with other salsas, then set aside.

When Victorian women grew bored during the long, dreary winter months, they often entertained themselves with catalogs. Catalogs for seed companies were designed largely for women, who did much of the gardening, so were flowery, elegant publications. Today, prints from those catalogs are often used as wall decorations.

Natural Cosmetics:
Almond - ground to a meal and often mixed with water to make a paste. It has soothing properties as well as some bleaching effects.
Aloe Vera - called the "burn plant" because of its healing properties. Used as a moisturizer or emollient.
Beeswax - used as an emulsifier in natural cosmetics. Some feel it clogs the pores.
Chamomile - when applied externally, this flower reduces puffiness and cleans the pores.
Lanolin - a natural moisturizer taken from sheep skin.
Vinegars - a final rinse to hair and skin for restoring proper PH. Must be diluted 1:1 with water.

- Cut salmon into six 8 ounce fillets, with outer skin remaining. Heat grill and brush with virgin olive oil.
- Cook salmon, skin side up first, for about 4 minutes per side.
- To serve, place salmon on three corn husks on plate. Pour salsa in three parallel diagonal lines across the top of salmon. Sauces should be side by side, but not mixing together. Garnish with cayenne pepper.

Serves 6.

Grilled Idaho Rainbow Trout Pancetta with Red Pepper Cream Sauce

for pancetta and trout:
fresh Idaho rainbow trout, 1 per person
1/4 slice pancetta per fish serving, chopped
3 Tablespoons extra virgin olive oil, approximate
edible flowers and fresh herbs, for garnish

for Roasted Red Pepper Sauce:
4 red bell peppers
3 cloves shallots
1 teaspoon fresh garlic, minced
1 teaspoon fresh thyme, minced
1 teaspoon fresh dill, minced
1 teaspoon lemon juice
1 Tablespoon heavy cream
salt and pepper, to taste

- Roast peppers and shallots under a broiler, turning frequently, until pepper skins darken significantly. Remove from the broiler.
- Place peppers into a paper sack. Close sack tightly and let sit for about 30 minutes to allow pepper skins to loosen.
- Peel peppers and purée in a food processor with shallots, garlic, thyme, dill, lemon juice, cream, salt, and pepper. Strain mixture through a mesh. Set aside in a warm place.
- Sauté pancetta until suitably cooked, nicely browned. Remove pancetta and set aside.
- Add the olive oil to the oils produced while sautéing the pancetta. Grill the trout, basting regularly with the oil mixture. Be careful not to overcook the fish.
- To serve, place the grilled trout on a warmed plate. Add sauce. Sprinkle pancetta on top. Garnish with edible flowers and fresh herbs.

Mary, Mary
Quite Contrary,
How does your
garden grow?
With silver bells, and
cockleshells, and pretty
maids all in a row.

When grilling or baking fish, it is best not to turn it. It falls apart easily.

Marinated Grilled Rabbit with Basil Cream Sauce

for rabbit:
fresh rabbit, cleaned and cut
squash blossoms, thoroughly washed
fresh zucchini
extra virgin olive oil
salt and pepper, to taste

for marinade:
3 to 4 cups white wine
6 cloves garlic, crushed
1 cup Tamari
1/4 cup extra virgin olive oil
2 Tablespoons brown sugar
a liberal amount of fresh rosemary, uncut

for Basil Cream Sauce:
1 cup fresh basil leaves
2 Tablespoons scallions, finely chopped (white part only)
1 Tablespoon fresh squeezed lemon juice
1 cup fresh butter
1 cup heavy cream
5 Tablespoons water
salt and pepper, to taste

- Mix all the marinade ingredients together. Marinate rabbit for 6 to 24 hours, turning occasionally. Save the marinade.
- Preheat oven to 350°. In a roasting pan, pre-cook rabbit for 30 minutes, basting occasionally with the marinade.
- Heat grill and cook rabbit until done, approximately 4 minutes per side. Baste frequently with the marinade.
- Place scallions, lemon juice, and water into a small sauté pan over medium heat. Add salt and pepper to taste and reduce until only

Rabbit is considered by many to be a very elegant, special occasion dish. Yet, because it is easy to raise, many country folk enjoy it regularly.

Rabbit was once a more common dish than it is today. Many old cookbooks will have 4 or 5 rabbit recipes.

This dish is great as an appetizer or on a buffet table.

- Christi

about 2 teaspoons of liquid remain.
- In the meantime, melt the butter over simmering water in the top part of a double boiler. When butter is liquefied, strain in the reduced liquid from the sauté pan.
- Slowly stir in the cream until the sauce is hot and completely blended. Season with salt and pepper.
- Place the basil into a food processor and purée thoroughly. Add the cream sauce to the processor and blend well. Strain the resulting mixture.
- Toss the squash blossoms in olive oil, salt, and pepper. Place the blossoms briefly into a hot oven until the blossoms just wilt.
- Split the zucchini into 1/8 inch to 1/4 inch julienne strips. Sauté the zucchini in olive oil and season to taste with salt and pepper.
- To serve, cover the bottom of the plate with Basil Cream Sauce and place rabbit on it. Arrange the zucchini and squash blossoms to the side of the meat.

Serves 4.

Rabbit is similar in flavor to chicken, so many recipes for the two are interchangeable. Rabbit has less fat than chicken, so it will need to be basted, even if the chicken recipe you use does not call for it. Because rabbits have scent glands that must be removed before cooking, I recommend you buy a dressed rabbit.

- Christi

Grilled Filet Mignon with Cognac Cream Sauce

for steaks:
fillet mignon, 1 per person
extra virgin olive oil
2 cloves garlic, crushed
salt and pepper, to taste

for Cognac Cream Sauce:
8 large egg yolks
4 Tablespoons sugar
1 cup Cognac
1 cup heavy cream
1 Tablespoon sweet butter
2 Tablespoons water

- Rub each steak with garlic and olive oil. Season with salt and pepper.
- Combine the egg yolks, cream, Cognac, water, and sugar in the top of a double boiler set over simmering water. Stirring constantly, heat the mixture for about 9 minutes or until the sauce thickens slightly. Do not boil.
- Add the butter and melt thoroughly. Keep the sauce in a warm place until ready to use.
- Grill the steaks over a medium hot fire.
- Drizzle the steaks with Cognac Cream Sauce before serving.

The more I study the world, the more I am convinced of the inability of brute force to create anything durable.
... Napoleon

A garden site should be planned to shelter plants from the wind. A garden near a building may be warmer, but be careful not to choose a spot with too much shade. Small fences or hedging are often used to protect the garden without shading it.

Grilled Rack of Lamb with Honey / Mustard Sauce

for lamb:
fresh rack of lamb
2 Tablespoons parsley, chopped
2 Tablespoons sage, chopped
2 Tablespoons rosemary, chopped
2 Tablespoons thyme, chopped
juice of 2 lemons
salt and pepper, to taste
edible flowers for garnish

for Honey / Mustard Sauce:
1 cup white wine
3 shallots, chopped
3 cloves garlic, crushed
3 cups heavy cream
3 Tablespoons Dijon mustard
2 Tablespoons pure clover honey
salt and pepper, to taste

The rack of the lamb comes just before the loin. It is the cut of meat consisting of all the rib chops in one piece, or the two rib roasts still attached. An average rack will weigh 3 to 4 pounds and will serve 4 people.

- Christi

- Salt and pepper rack of lamb, then roll the rack in a mixture of the chopped herbs until it is well coated. Grill the rack, basting occasionally with lemon juice, until cooked.
- Place wine, shallots, and garlic into a saucepan. Reduce over medium high heat until just 2 Tablespoons of liquid remain.
- Add cream and reduce slowly over medium high heat until the mixture reduces to half of its former volume, about 2 cups.
- Pour mixture into a food processor and blend.
- Add the mustard and honey. Blend well. Salt and pepper to taste. Strain through a mesh.
- To serve, cut the rack into serving pieces. Place sauce onto warmed plates and position meat on the plates. Sprinkle lightly with any remaining chopped herbs. Garnish with edible flowers.

Marinated Grilled Lamb with Stuffed Nasturtiums and Raspberry / Mustard Glaze

fresh lamb, any cut

for marinade:
3 to 4 cups white wine
6 cloves garlic, crushed
1 cup Tamari
1/4 cup extra virgin olive oil
2 Tablespoons brown sugar
a liberal amount of fresh rosemary, uncut

for Raspberry / Mustard Glaze:
4 Tablespoons honey
4 ounces Dijon mustard
1 cube unsalted butter
1/4 cup fresh raspberries
dash of fresh lemon juice
dash of sugar

for nasturtiums:
nasturtiums blossoms, well washed
1/2 cup fresh chevre
1/2 teaspoon fresh squeezed lemon juice
1 Tablespoon fresh parsley, chopped
1/4 cup fresh raspberries
1/2 teaspoon sugar, or to taste
salt and pepper, to taste

- Mix together all the marinade ingredients. Marinade lamb for 6 to 24 hours, turning occasionally. Save marinade.
- Preheat oven to 350°. In a roasting pan, precook lamb for 30 minutes, basting occasionally with marinade.
- Heat grill and cook lamb until done, about 4 minutes per side. Baste frequently with marinade. Reserve remaining marinade.

In Europe, as well as at Hotel Carter, summer salads often have nasturtiums. The leaves can be chopped fine and used like parsley, whole flowers added after the salad has been tossed.

- Christi

- Strain marinade to remove rough herbs. Reduce over a high heat until it is about half its original volume. Remove from heat.
- Add honey and mustard. Whip sauce and slowly add butter piece by piece. The sauce should still be warm enough to melt butter without returning the sauce to the heat when butter is added in small portions.

- While butter is melting, purée raspberries with lemon juice and sugar. Strain to remove seeds. Add resulting mixture to honey / mustard mixture. Mix well. Keep warm.
- Toss together chevre, lemon juice, parsley, raspberries, sugar, salt, and pepper.
- Stuff nasturtium blossoms with above filling mixture. Warm briefly in a hot oven.
  To serve, cover a warm plate with Raspberry
- Mustard Glaze and place lamb on it. Arrange stuffed nasturtiums on a plate and drizzle a bit more of the glaze over the meat.

Tree roots can steal valuable nutrients from the garden. Avoid siting a garden too near to large trees.

Stuffed Rock Cornish Game Hens with Fresh Sage Sauce

for game hens:
6 rock cornish game hens
6 cloves garlic, cut into slivers
2 teaspoons fresh thyme leaves, chopped
6 fresh sage leaves, chopped
homemade poultry stuffing, your favorite (an example is on the facing page)
extra virgin olive oil
salt and pepper, to taste
deep fried sage leaves (recipe in margin)

for Fresh Sage Sauce:
1 cup white wine
1 yellow onion, chopped
3 cloves garlic, chopped
2 cups heavy cream
8 to 10 fresh sage leaves

Deep Fried Sage Leaves:
Place 1/2 cup of olive oil in a frying pan and heat. Add 8 to 10 sage leaves and fry until crispy. Drain on a paper towel.

- Make your favorite stuffing.
- Preheat oven to 350°. Work garlic, thyme, and sage around and in-between the meat and the skin, primarily the breast portion.
- Stuff the hens. Coat outside of skin of game hen with extra virgin olive oil and sprinkle with salt and pepper. Bake for about 40 minutes or until cooked to your preference.
- Place wine, onion, and garlic into a pan and reduce over high heat until 1 Tablespoon of liquid remains.
- Add 2 cups heavy cream. Reduce over lower heat until thickened.
- Place cream sauce and sage leaves into a food processor. Process until thick and creamy. The leaves will remain somewhat chunky.
- To serve, place game hens on plate. Drizzle a few spoonfuls of sage sauce over it. Garnish with deep fried sage leaves.

Marinated Grilled Quail with Grilled Pears and Wilted Fresh Greens

for quail:
fresh quail, halved
fresh baby greens, variety of your choice
fresh sage, chopped
extra virgin olive oil
pancetta
pears, halved

for marinade:
3 to 4 cups white wine
6 cloves garlic, crushed
1 cup Tamari
1/4 cup extra virgin olive oil
3 Tablespoons brown sugar
a liberal amount of fresh rosemary, uncut

- Mix together all marinade ingredients. Marinate quail for 6 to 24 hours. Turn often.
- Grill the quail until cooked, basting regularly with marinade. Reserve marinade.
- When the quail is almost ready to be removed from the grill, place the pear halves onto the grill and baste with oil. Grill the pears briefly on both sides, until fruit is tender.
- In a large skillet, sauté pancetta with the fresh sage. When cooked, remove and drain the mixture on paper towels. Reserve the pancetta oil in the pan.
- Add some additional olive oil to the pan and heat the oils. When the oils are hot, toss in the baby greens and cook until just wilted.
- To serve, arrange a bed of wilted greens on a plate and top with half a quail. Cover the quail with the pancetta/sage mixture. Arrange pears to the side of the quail.

In the South, where Michael and I were raised, the best dishes are the ones taken to pot lucks, usually for church socials and family get-togethers. A favorite ingredient is cream of mushroom soup.

My favorite stuffing recipe is one I learned at my mamma's knee. The ingredients are:

1 small cornbread round
8 slices whole grain bread
3 stalks celery, chopped
1 cup pecans, chopped
1 onion, chopped
2 cans cream of mushroom soup
3 Tablespoons sage
1 Tablespoon thyme
1/2 cup butter, melted
water, added last to give it the right consistency

Break breads into small pieces. Mix in a large bowl with all other ingredients. Bake in a 350° oven for 45 minutes or until lightly browned.

Chiffonade of Fresh Greens

fresh Swiss chard
fresh red Swiss chard
fresh mustard greens
fresh beet greens
salt and pepper, to taste
clarified butter OR white wine/garlic sauce

A little honey or sugar will bring out the flavor in fresh vegetables more than salt will. A favorite snack is to take a room temperature fresh tomato, cut it into thick slices and sprinkle it with honey, chives, and pepper. This is especially good with cottage cheese or fresh bread.

- Rinse well all the greens and dry thoroughly
- Stack leaves vertically and roll. Cut rolled greens into 1/8 inch to 1/4 inch slices.
- Sauté very briefly, just a few seconds, over high heat in clarified butter or wine/garlic mixture. Serve immediately.

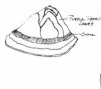

Baby Artichokes

fresh baby artichokes
fresh lemon
extra virgin olive oil OR melted butter
lemon juice

- Cut stems and tops from artichokes. Trim ti off all leaves.
- Rub artichokes with fresh lemon and place pot of boiling water. Reduce heat and simm artichokes for 20 - 30 minutes or until tende
- Before serving, brush artichokes with olive or melted butter and lemon juice.

Grilled Baby Vegetables

It is true the simple dishes are often the best ones. It is not unusual for our guests to compliment the main dish the chef has labored over, but rave about these simple grilled vegetables. They are easy to do, but the guests appreciate them as much as anything we serve. The same process can be used for many vegetables, use your imagination and creativity, but I have listed our favorite ones here.

for basting sauce:
1 clove garlic, crushed
1/2 cup extra virgin olive oil
salt and pepper, to taste

for vegetables:
baby leeks OR snow peas OR baby summer squash OR fresh slices of tri-colored bell peppers OR baby zucchini
a combination of two of the above is also good

- Grill vegetable until tender, brushing occasionally with basting sauce.
- Season with salt and pepper to taste and any fresh herbs you might want to add.

An artichoke is a perennial vegetable with landscape value. A big, ferny-looking plant, the form is irregular and the leaves are silvery green. Big flower buds form at the top of the stalks, which are the artichokes you cook and eat. If not cut, the buds open into a beautiful purple-blue thistle-like flower. These plants like cool weather.

Purée of Fresh Fennel and Broccoli

1 head fresh broccoli
1 head fresh fennel
1 medium onion OR chopped garlic
3 Tablespoons assorted fresh herbs, your choice
clarified butter
1/4 cup heavy cream
salt and pepper, to taste

Fennel is a perennial herb, usually grown as a summer annual. The young leaves and seeds have a slight licorice taste. The plants often grow as roadside or garden weeds. They are attractive until the tops turn brown, but even then the seeds are a favorite food of wild birds.

- Slice broccoli, stems optional, and par boil for about 3 minutes.
- Slice fennel and par boil for about 5 minutes or until tender.
- While both broccoli and fennel are still warm, purée together in a food processor with the heavy cream.
- Chop onion, or garlic, and sauté over high heat in clarified butter until golden brown, almost caramelized.
- Add onion to broccoli/fennel mixture and purée again until all of the ingredients are well mixed.
- Mix fresh herbs together. Add to purée and toss together well.

Quinoa Timbales

quinoa
salt and pepper, to taste
Tamari
3 Tablespoons fresh herbs, your choice, 1
    Tablespoon each

- Boil pot of water and add grain. Simmer for about 20 minutes on low heat.
- Remove from heat and season with salt, pepper, Tamari, and your selection of herbs. Toss together.
- Pack quinoa mixture in timbale cups and place in pan of hot water. Cover pan with foil. Keep in warm oven until ready to serve.
- To serve, turn timbales upside down on serving plates and tap to remove.

As America's taste for meat lessens, grains and beans are finding new respect in the market place. Quinoa is one of several grains gaining popularity in the United States. It can be served like rice, or used as a base for a salad. Quinoa is from South America and has a sweet flavor and soft texture.

Summer Squash Timbale

4 cups young summer squash, a variety is best,
   finely chopped or grated
1 yellow onion, finely chopped
1 teaspoon garlic, minced
2 Tablespoons extra virgin olive oil
3 Tablespoons mixed fresh herbs, your choice
5 eggs, beaten
2 cups heavy cream
butter, for greasing molds
1 cup dry french bread crumbs
1 cup parmesan cheese, freshly grated
salt and pepper, to taste
fresh herb sprigs, for garnish

A timbale is a molded vegetable custard.

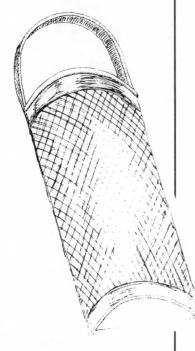

In ancient times, breaking long loaves of bread represented breaking swords and was meant as a sign of peace.

- Place squash in a colander set over a bowl or in a sink. Generously sprinkle with salt, mix with fingertips to distribute salt evenly. Let stand for 30 minutes.
- Gather squash in your hand and gently squeeze to release any additional surface moisture. Set aside.
- Heat olive oil in skillet over medium high heat. Add onion and sauté until soft, about minutes. Add the garlic and sauté 1 minute longer.
- Remove from the heat and toss onion/garlic mixture with squash. Add the minced herbs and mix well.
- Mix in the eggs and cream. Season to taste with salt and pepper.
- Preheat oven to 350°. Butter the bottom and sides of a 5 cup mold or 10 1/2 cup metal timbale molds or ceramic custard cups.
- Dust molds with bread crumbs to coat completely. Shake out excess crumbs.
- Fill the crumb lined containers with the squash mixture. Place the containers in a baking pan with enough hot water to reach

two-thirds up the sides of the containers.
- Bake timbales, uncovered, until they set, about 1 hour for a large mold or 30 minutes for smaller ones.
- Remove timbales from the oven and let stand about 5 minutes.
- Run a thin-blade knife or spatula around the inside edge of the mold and invert containers onto a platter or individual serving plates.
- Before serving, sprinkle with parmesan cheese and garnish with fresh herbs.

Makes 10-12 timbales.

Squash is an annual that comes in two forms. Summer squash is harvested in the immature state and includes white squash, yellow crookneck, and zucchini or Italian squash. Winter varieties have hard rinds and firm, fine-flavored flesh. They are usually baked or made into pies. They come in many shapes and store well.

Cucumber Boats

Excellent as either a garniture or hors d'oeuvres. Begin with tender, young cucumbers. Remove the ends then cut into short pieces (1 1/2" - 2") long. Cut pieces in half lengthwise.

Make a lengthwise cut parallel to the center leaving about 1/4 of the slice still attached. Scoop out the seeds to form the hull.

Pull the sliced top back to form a sail and use a toothpick as a mast. The hull may then be filled with caviar, cheese mixture, dressing, or dip. Great for seafood dishes.

Stuffed Summer Squash

1 pound new potatoes
3 Tablespoons unsalted butter, melted
1/2 cup heavy cream
2 Tablespoons extra virgin olive oil
1/2 cup yellow onion, finely chopped
3 cups fresh summer squash, chopped
6 small squash, whole
1 teaspoon garlic, minced
2 Tablespoons fresh parsley, minced
1 Tablespoon fresh chives, minced
1 teaspoon fresh sage, minced
1 teaspoon fresh thyme, minced
salt and pepper, to taste
fresh herb sprigs and edible flowers, for garnish

Every kitchen needs a long butcher's steel for sharpening knives. They are easy to find; any store which sells quality knives will have them.

To sharpen the blade, press the knife edge against the steel at a 20° angle. Starting with the heel of the blade at the top of the steel, draw the blade across and down to the bottom of the steel in a short easy swinging motion. Repeat several times, then repeat on the other side.

- Preheat oven to 325°.
- Cut off and reserve the tops of the 6 small squash. With spoon, scoop out squash centers and reserve.
- Rub squash shells and tops with olive oil inside and out. Season to taste with salt and pepper. Add minced garlic.
- Bake the squash shells and tops in a covered baking dish for about 20 minutes, or until squash are tender but still hold their shapes.
- Boil potatoes until tender. Drain and purée with butter and cream in a food processor.
- Over medium high heat, sauté onions and garlic in olive oil for about 5 minutes.
- Add the removed squash centers and chopped squash and continue to sauté for 1 minutes or until squash is very tender.
- Add the squash sauté to potato purée and blend well. Mix in the parsley, chives, sage, and thyme. Season with salt and pepper.
- Stuff the squash shells with warm squash filling. Garnish with herb sprigs and flowers.

Serves 6.

Winter Squash Fritters

1 fresh winter squash, approximately 2 pounds
1/4 cup heavy cream
4 Tablespoons corn starch
2 large eggs
4 Tablespoons fresh herbs, your choice
1 Tablespoon garlic, chopped
salt and pepper, to taste
olive oil, for frying
crème fraîche

- Peel, de-seed, and shred squash.
- Place shreds in mixing bowl with cream, corn starch, eggs, salt, pepper, herbs, and garlic. Toss mixture together until well combined.
- Heat griddle and lubricate with small amount of olive oil.
- Pour batter into circles, pancake style, and fry the fritters until golden brown, about 1 minute per side.
- Dab fritters with crème fraîche and serve immediately.

Dover Egg-Beater

When dried flowers become dusty, pour a couple of handfuls of table salt into a paper bag, place the flowers head-first into the bag and gently stir them through the salt.

The menus at Carter House and Hotel Carter change frequently. There are dishes that we serve as appetizers at banquets or receptions and as entrees at the hotel. Some pastries are served with breakfast and also as dessert at dinner. Here are some of our favorite combinations with the page numbers of the recipes.
            - Christi & Mark

**Marinated Grilled Rabbit
with Basil Cream Sauce**
- page 96 -
Fresh Corn / Butternut Squash Soup
- page 68 -
Merlot Sorbet
- page 143 -
Grilled Salmon with Tri-Colored Salsa
- page 92 -
Chiffonade of Fresh Greens
- page 104 -
**Raspberry Mousse in
Brandy Snap Baskets**
- page 140 -

**Fresh Baked Oysters
with Spinach and Herbs**
- page 58 -
Cream of Asparagus Soup
- page 75 -
Minted Grapefruit Sorbet
- page 143 -
**Grilled Rack of Lamb
with Honey / Mustard Sauce**
- page 99 -
Quinoa Timbales
- page 107 -
Grilled Baby Vegetables
- page 105 -
Chocolate Mint Roulade
- page 136 -

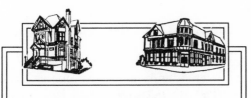

**Marinated Grilled Quail
with Grilled Pears**
- page 103 -
Black Bean and Pumpkin Soup
- page 66 -
Orange Chive Sorbet
- page 142 -
Grilled Idaho Rainbow Trout
- page 95 -
Stuffed Summer Squash
- page 110 -
Apple Blueberry Cream Puff
- page 134 -

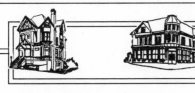

**Duck Sausage with Polenta
and Wild Blackberry Sauce**
- page 56 -
**Fresh Pea Soup
with Mint Crème Fraîche**
- page 74 -
Pinot Noir Oregano Sorbet
- page 144 -
**Filet Mignon
with Cognac Cream Sauce**
- page 98 -
Winter Squash Fritters
- page 111 -
**Strawberry Meringue Torte
with Apricot Sauce**
- page 138 -

One of the things our guests tell us over and over is that a dinner at Hotel Carter is an event. We appreciate those comments because that is what we aspire to present. Although it may be more difficult to serve a daily five course meal at home, there are several times throughout the year when a certain panache is called for. We hope there are some ideas here that will make your next birthday, holiday, family reunion, or anniversary a special, intimate event.

- Christi & Mark

John's Wine Selections and Food Recommendations

This list is neither all inclusive nor exclusive. One of the perks of my position is that I have access to some of the best food and wines in the country. I recommend what I like. If all the wines listed are not available to you, hopefully the descriptions of the wines will help you make a selection from your area.

1988 Stag's Leap Sauvignon Blanc (Napa) - a dry, crisp, yet fruity wine with a slightly herbaceous flavor. I recommend this wine with the Baked Oysters with Spinach because it resonates especially well with the herbs.

1987 Clos Du Val Chardonnay (Napa) - a very dry chardonnay with just a hint of oak, high acid, good fruitiness, rich and buttery. This wine has a nice "apple" quality and an excellent floral bouquet that compliment the Grilled Prawns exceptionally well.

1988 Fieldbrook Dry Chenin Blanc (Humboldt) - a favorite local wine, dry, yet fruity, with an excellent clean finish. The fruity nose plus the light clean finish is an excellent compliment to the Smoked Salmon Medallions.

1987 Clos Du Bois Merlot (Sonoma) - an outstanding wine. The tannins are mellow; the flavor full bodied; the finish leaves a sensuous hint of wood on the tongue. When served with the Grilled Rabbit in Basil Cream Sauce, the wine is light enough to gracefully compliment the rabbit, yet strong enough to provide a sturdy counterpoint to the basil sauce.

1987 Madrona Vineyards Johannesburg Riesling (Placer) - this is a dry, low-sugar riesling with a magnificent floral bouquet. The floral characteristics of the wine seem to unify the various flavors found in the Grilled Quail with Pancetta.

1987 Gundlach-Bundschu Gewurtztraminer (Sonoma) - this is a dry Gewurtztraminer with a lot of floral characteristics - it suits the Tri-Colored Salmon quite nicely. The many gustatory nuances created with the three salsa provide an array of flavors for the wine to work with, which it does quite well.

1980 Robert Mondavi Reserve Cabernet Sauvignon (Napa) - Every true meat lover can appreciate the perfectly cooked steak with the perfectly aged, powerhouse red wine. This wine is powerful, bold, rich yet well mannered, perfectly balanced, a Mercedes of wines, excellent with the Filet Mignon.

1986 Robert Stemmier Pinot Noir (Sonoma) - a very nice pinot, fairly light. The wild and spicy flavors of the Apple, Sausage, Sage Sauté become loosely draped by this wine. The relative sweetness works well with the apple and the pinot even enlivens the butteriness of the phyllo pastry.

Over dessert one night, we asked Mark to tell us some of his favorite innkeeper stories, humorous and otherwise. Except for a good bottle of wine, nothing seems to bring light heartedness to the table better than a sweet treat. We asked Mark to tell us about some of his unusual or famous guests. Had any movie stars come to stay at Carter House or Hotel Carter?

Mark confided that yes, he does see his share of famous people. But mostly, they are guests from the college; musicians, newscasters, politicians, historians, writers, and visionaries. He laughed and said he enjoys meeting these people, but often feels inadequate to converse with some of the luminary minds that sit in his parlor. However, one guest put him at ease in that respect.

A well known musician from the flower power era came to stay at Hotel Carter while doing a gig at a bar, just a few blocks from the hotel. After his night's performance, he had difficulty finding his way back. He called a cab but could not remember where he was staying. After driving around for a bit, the cab driver took him to another hotel where he checked in for the night. The next morning, the singer returned to the hotel for breakfast.

"When I asked him how he liked the room," Mark said, "He said he didn't know. He didn't sleep there."

Then Mark told us a story which did not happen at Hotel Carter, but in a restaurant not far away. A talkative female guest was sharing dinner with a very detached male friend. The waiter became suspicious about the man's remoteness and discreetly called the manager over to investigate. Realizing the man had died at the table, the manager agonized over how to tell the woman the news. He finally approached the table and gently interrupted her.

"I am sorry, madam," he said. "I am afraid your friend has suddenly passed away."

The woman stared in disbelief at the manager, then looked at her companion and snapped angrily, "Well then, who is going to pay the bill?"

But Mark's best story involves another hotel. Just before dawn an elderly woman crept anxiously into the lobby of a local establishment. She tearfully confessed that her companion had died and she did not know what to do. The desk clerk looked up from his paper and asked, "Did he eat here tonight?"

Now we have heard the expression, food worth dying for, but we do not think that is how the clerk meant it. It is a phrase, however, that has been used when describing Christi's desserts. We will, of course, let you decide for yourself.

Puff Pastry Dough

3 cups pastry flour, sifted before measuring
1 Tablespoon unsalted butter, softened
3/4 cup water, ice cold
juice of 1 lemon
1/2 to 3/4 pound unsalted butter, cold

- Place the flour into a large bowl. Work in the soft butter with a pastry blender.
- Make a well in the center and pour in the ice cold water and lemon juice. Work the mixture with the tips of your fingers until you have a crumbly, but somewhat cohesive, ball. Cover the mixture and refrigerate for at least 1 hour.
- Roll out the cold dough into a square, 1/2 inch thick.
- Remove the cold butter from the refrigerator and hit it with a rolling pin to soften it. Crumble the butter and sprinkle it on <u>one half</u> of the rolled out dough.
- Fold the half of the dough that is not covered with butter over the half that is, making sure that the edges are even with each other. The dough should now be in a rectangular shape. Lightly press together the two layers.
- Roll over the rectangle toward the folded edge. Roll in light even strokes to keep the butter from oozing out.
- When the dough is stretched, fold it in thirds, like a letter you are folding to put in an envelope. Place the dough on a sheet of foil and refrigerate for 1 hour or more.
- Place the dough on a floured surface with the open edge away from you. Roll into a rectangle the same as before. Once again, fold the dough into thirds like a letter. Refrigerate for 30 minutes or more.
- Repeat the roll, fold, and chill process at least

Puff pastry dough is not difficult to make, just time consuming. I like to make a large amount at once, planning the day around the process, then freezing the dough for later use. While the dough is in the chilling stage, I wash clothes, read, or catch up on correspondence.
- Christi

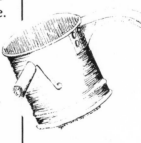

HANDLED CASSEROLE
INDIVIDUAL SIZE

The principal ingredients of all pastry crusts are flour, fat, and liquid. The differences in crusts come from the proportions and the methods of combining ingredients.

three more times, chilling the dough for 30 minutes or more each time. After the final rolling, wrap in plastic wrap and refrigerate overnight.

- The next day, roll half or all of the cold dough into a sheet 1/4 inch thick. Cut into shapes according to your needs. Freeze what you will not need.
- Puff pastry is baked in a preheated oven at 450° for 25 minutes or according to the directions of a particular recipe.

Almond Phyllo Tart

for pastry:
8 sheets phyllo dough, thawed if frozen
1/4 pound unsalted butter, melted
1/2 cup almonds, finely ground
powdered sugar

for filling:
1/2 cup unsalted butter, softened
1/2 cup sugar
1 egg
2 Tablespoons dark rum
2 teaspoons almond extract
2 Tablespoons all-purpose flour
2 1/2 cups finely ground blanched almonds

- Cream the butter and sugar for the filling with an electric mixer. Add egg, rum, almond extract, and flour. Beat until smooth. Fold in the almonds.
- Preheat oven to 350°.
- Lay a phyllo sheet across a 9 inch tart pan with removable bottom. Brush with melted butter and sprinkle with almonds. Repeat this procedure with the remaining sheets, stacking one on top of the other.
- Spread the filling in the last sheet to fit the dimensions of the pan. Gently fold the edges of each sheet back toward the center of the pan, brushing with melted butter as you go.
- Bake for 30 to 35 minutes.
- Cool. Dust with powdered sugar.

When I was 12, Uncle Ralph was managing a hotel in the Virgin Islands. James Brown came for a show and Ralph sent us the publicity shot of him welcoming the entertainer to the hotel. I carried that photo around until it was dog-eared. My uncle had met James Brown! Now that was exciting. My parents were not into the music, so they were not impressed. None the less, they asked him about famous people he had met. Ralph always obliged us with a dropped name or two, mostly people we had never heard of. Then he would tell a story about a local eccentric he knew who was just as interesting. Perhaps famous people are interesting to us because they are visibly following their dreams. But all around us are other people whose dreams are not quite so obvious. I know several waiters with a Masters degree. People are not always what they seem to be.

Toasted Almond Torte with Raspberries and Gran Marnier Creme Anglaise

for Gran Marnier Creme Anglaise:
2 cups heavy cream
1 vanilla bean, split in half lengthwise
4 large egg yolks
3/4 cup granulated sugar
3 to 5 Tablespoons Gran Marnier

for torte:
1 1/2 cups cake flour
1 teaspoon baking powder
1 cup sugar
1 cup sweet butter
8 ounces natural almond paste
1/4 cup toasted almonds, finely ground
4 eggs
1 teaspoon real vanilla extract
fresh raspberries, for layering on torte
heavy cream, gently whipped, for layering on torte
lavender blooms, for garnishing

- In a saucepan over medium heat, bring crea
  and vanilla bean for Creme Anglaise to a boil,
  stirring frequently to prevent scorching.
- In a bowl, using a wire whisk, beat egg yolk
  and sugar together until creamy and light
  yellow in color, 2 to 3 minutes. Whisking
  continually, add the boiling vanilla/cream
  mixture.
- Return the resulting mixture to the saucepai
  Stirring continuously with a wooden spoon,
  heat over low heat until mixture is thick
  enough to coat the spoon, 30 to 60 seconds.
- Pour the Creme Anglaise through a fine
  mesh sieve into a stainless steel or glass
  container. Mix in the Gran Marnier to taste.

Before measuring butter or shortening, dip the measuring spoon into hot water. The fat won't stick to a heated spoon.

Tell me what you eat and I will tell you who you are.
... Anthelme Brillat-Savarin

- Let mixture cool to room temperature. Store, covered, in the refrigerator.
- Preheat oven to 350°. Lightly grease the bottom of a 9 inch spring-form pan, then line the bottom with a circle of parchment paper. Lightly grease and flour the rest of the pan and paper.
- Sift flour and baking powder together. Set aside.
- In a large bowl, cream together sugar, butter, and almond paste until light and airy.
- Add eggs, one at a time, beating well after each addition. Next, stir in the vanilla and ground almonds.
- Fold in flour/baking powder until mixture is smooth and creamy.
- Pour batter into a prepared cake pan. Bake until golden, about 40 to 50 minutes. A wooden skewer inserted into the center of the torte should pull out clean.
- Cool the torte for 10 minutes in the pan. Remove. Cool on rack until torte assumes room temperature. Once cooled, sift a heavy layer of powdered sugar on top of the torte.
- To serve, cover bottom of an individual serving plate with Gran Marnier Creme Anglaise. Place a slice of the torte onto the plate. Place a dollop of gently whipped cream onto the slice of torte. Pile raspberries to the side of the torte and garnish with fresh lavender blooms.

Raspberries will grow almost anywhere in the western United States, but require a slowly warming, lingering spring to reach perfection. The word's origins come from Old High German, hrespan, meaning to rack together, possibly referring to the berry clusters.

Apple Almond Tart
Carter House

This recipe appeared in Gourmet magazine in October of 1988. One taste will reveal why this is our most famous recipe.

for the crust:
1 1/4 cups all-purpose flour
1 stick unsalted butter, cut into pieces
2 Tablespoons sugar
1 large egg

for the almond mixture:
3/4 cup sliced almonds, toasted lightly
1/2 cup sugar
2 Tablespoons unsalted butter
1 large egg

for topping:
1 large Granny Smith apple
1/3 cup apricot jam, heat and strained
2 Tablespoons Triple Sec

According to *In Health* magazine, it takes 3 minutes each day to separate an average household's paper, glass, and aluminum for recycling. Paper will decompose in 1 month in a landfill. Glass and aluminum decompose in 500 years.

- In a food processor, blend the flour, butter, and sugar until the mixture resembles coarse meal. Add the egg and blend the mixture until it just forms a soft dough.
- Roll the dough into an 11 inch round on a lightly floured surface and fit the round carefully into a 9 inch pan with a removable fluted rim.
- Preheat oven to 375°.
- In a food processor, grind finely the almonds with the sugar. Add the butter and the egg. Blend the mixture until it is smooth. Spread the almond mixture evenly on the crust.
- Peel, core, and slice very thinly the apple. Arrange it on the almond mixture. Bake the

tart in the middle of the preheated oven for 25 to 30 minutes, or until the crust is golden.
- Transfer the tart to a rack and let it cool.
- In a small bowl, whisk together the jam and the Triple Sec. Brush the glaze over the cooled tart.

The Fleurs-de-lys

Fold napkin diagonally in half to form a triangle.

Fold base of triangle up half way to form a hat shape.

Fold 1/3 of the hat brim down.

Pleat the napkin across from left to right.

Place in glass, open the napkin out and arrange as shown in drawing.

Storage Time for Home-Frozen Fruit:

Apples, sliced
   best- less than 6 mo.
   fair - less than 12 mo.

Peaches, sliced
   best - less than 6 mo.
   fair - less than 24 mo.

Cherries
   best - less than 12 mo.
   fair - less than 24 mo.

Strawberries
   best - less than 4 mo.
   fair - less than 6 mo.

Fruits freeze well in freezer bags. Then you can see what is inside and its condition.

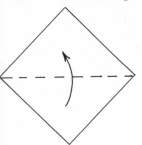

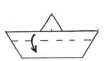

Handmade Coffee Gelato with Creme Anglaise

for Creme Anglaise:
2 cups heavy cream
1 vanilla bean, split in half lengthwise
4 large egg yolks
3/4 cup granulated sugar

for gelato:
1 cup heavy cream
1 cup milk
3/4 cup sugar
1 cup extremely strong coffee, cool
pinch of salt

A gelato is an Italian ice cream. It is usually lighter because it contains no or few eggs.

A gourmet is just a glutton with brains.
... Phillip W. Haberman

- In a saucepan, bring cream and vanilla bean for Creme Anglaise to a boil, stirring frequently to prevent scorching.
- In a bowl, using a wire whisk, beat egg yolk and sugar until creamy and light yellow in color, 2 to 3 minutes. Whisking continually, add the boiling vanilla/cream mixture.
- Return the resulting mixture to the saucepan. Stirring continuously with a wooden spoon, heat over low heat until mixture is thick enough to coat the spoon, 30 to 60 seconds.
- Pour the Creme Anglaise through a fine sieve into a stainless steel or glass container.
- Let mixture cool to room temperature. Store, covered, in the refrigerator.
- Mix together all gelato ingredients, adding salt last after all other ingredients are mixed. Place mixture in ice cream maker and freeze according to manufacturer's specifications.
- To serve, place 2 scoops of gelato in each individual serving dish. Top with Creme Anglaise.

Homemade Lavender Ice Cream

Dessert fans and gourmands alike will be delighted with this ice cream made from flower petals. It is unique, alluring and, most importantly, delicious.

---

2 cup heavy cream
1 cup milk
1/2 cup sugar
1 vanilla bean, split and cut
1/3 cup fresh lavender petals

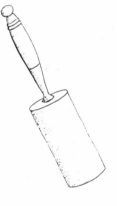

- Mix milk, cream, sugar, vanilla bean, and lavender petals in a deep saucepan. Scald milk over low heat, dissolving sugar, but not scorching.
- Cover and refrigerate for several hours.
- When flavor of mixture is strong enough, remove vanilla bean and lavender petals with a strainer.
- Pour strained mixture into an ice cream maker and freeze according to manufacturer's specifications.

Lavender is an evergreen shrub native to the Mediterranean region. Its fragrant flowers are used for perfumes and sachets and have a soothing effect.

Individual Hazelnut-Mocha Torte with Mocha Butter Cream and Mocha Sauce

The meal you serve has to be pretty impressive not to be overshadowed by this spectacular dessert!

---

for tortes:
1 cup hazelnuts, roasted and skinned
6 large egg whites
2 Tablespoons corn starch
3/4 cup sugar
1/2 teaspoon cream of tartar
1 cup hazelnuts, chopped, for garnish
chocolate shavings, for garnish
edible flowers, for garnish

---

for Mocha Butter Cream:
1 cup sugar
1 cup very strong instant coffee
3 to 4 Tablespoons Gran Marnier
6 egg yolks
1 pound sweet butter, room temperature

---

for Mocha Sauce:
2 cups heavy cream
1/4 cup very strong coffee or espresso
3 Tablespoons Gran Marnier

- Preheat oven to 350°. Grease an 11 X 17 inch cake pan and line with parchment paper.
- In a food processor, mix sugar, corn starch, and hazelnuts for tortes. Process until the mixture has the consistency of a fine powder.
- In a separate bowl, whip egg whites together with cream of tartar until they hold a nice peak. Fold powder mixture into egg whites and pour into the cake pan.
- Bake for 20 to 25 minutes, or until a toothpick

Torte or Tart? Generally, tarts are made like pies, tortes are closer to cakes.

"Eating humble pie" means to be humiliated. The saying comes from the days when the Lord of the Manor and his fellow huntsmen feasted on prime meat, while the servants had to make do with a pie made from the scraps.

inserted in the center comes out clean.
- Let cool and remove from cake pan onto another piece of parchment paper. Remove old parchment paper from the bottom of cake. Cut cake into 3 inch circles.
- With electric mixer, beat butter for Butter Cream until soft and creamy. Set aside.
- Combine sugar, coffee, and Gran Marnier and bring to a boil for three minutes.
- Using an electric mixer, beat egg yolks at medium speed, adding sugar/coffee/liqueur mixture <u>very slowly</u>. Beat ingredients together for 10 minutes, until the mixture assumes a mayonnaise texture. Add butter slowly and gently mix at medium speed.
- Combine all Mocha Sauce ingredients. Mix thoroughly with hand whisk.
- To serve, layer 3 cake circles with Mocha Butter Cream. Cover with chopped hazelnuts and serve with Mocha Sauce. Garnish with chocolate shavings and edible flowers.

Lemon Grass Lemonade:
Make a syrup from 3 stalks of fresh lemon grass. Cut off the leafy top and peel the tough outer layer. Discard discolored or dried out root ends. Cut the trimmed, woody sections into 2 inch lengths and crush with a hammer. Boil in a saucepan with 1 cup sugar and 1 cup water. Reduce to 1 cup liquid, about 30 minutes. Cool. Add the cup of syrup to 5 cups water and 6 Tablespoons lemon juice.

Kiwi Puff Pastry with Fresh Raspberry Sauce

for Kiwi Puffs:
puff pastry dough, 2 packages if frozen
6 sweet kiwis
1 Tablespoon water
1 egg yolk

for Fresh Raspberry Sauce:
2 cups fresh raspberries
1/2 cup sugar, to taste
juice of 1 lemon
4 Tablespoons Raspberry Liqueur

- Cover a baking sheet in parchment paper. Preheat oven to 400°.
- Peel kiwis and slice off tops and bottoms.
- Roll pastry dough into 1 large sheet 1/8 inch thick. Cut dough into strips approximately 1/2 inch wide by 1 foot long.
- Roll a continuous pastry strip around each kiwi. You may need to splice strips together with water, depending on the size of the fruit. Spiral the pastry from the bottom up, leaving 1/4 inch space between each pass of the pastry dough on the way up.
- Mix egg yolk and water in a bowl. Coat each wrapped kiwi with egg wash.
- Place kiwi puffs on baking sheet covered with parchment paper. Bake for 20 to 30 minutes until puffs are a nice golden brown. Let cool.
- Purée raspberries, sugar, lemon juice, and liqueur in a food processor until the desired sauce consistency is achieved. Strain sauce through a fine screen to remove seeds.
- To serve, place pastries on individual serving dishes. Pour a small amount of sauce over each pastry and garnish with edible flowers.

Companion Plants: To discourage pests, plant garlic, onions, and marigolds between rows of vegetables in the garden. Dill grows adjacent to beets and cabbage. Zinnias and flowering herbs encourage beneficial insects such as bees, for pollination, and praying mantises, which feed on aphids. Sunflowers can provide afternoon shade for heat sensitive plants such as carrots, cucumbers and late peas.

Mexican Toasted Almond Cookies

2 cups all purpose flour
3/4 cup confectioner's sugar, sifted
1 cup toasted almonds
1 teaspoon pure almond extract
1/2 pound sweet butter, softened
1/2 Tablespoon grated lemon peel
1/2 Tablespoon grated orange peel
1 pinch salt
1 pinch cinnamon

- Lightly oil a cookie baking sheet. Preheat oven to 350°.
- In a food processor, mix together the flour, 1/2 cup of the sugar, the nuts, salt, and cinnamon. Stir in the almond extract and the lemon and orange peels. Gradually work the butter in until a cohesive ball forms.
- Shape the dough into small patties. Place on the baking sheet and bake for 30 minutes, or until the cookies are delicately brown.
- Remove cookies from the oven and cool them on a wire rack. Dust them with the remaining confectioner's sugar.

A birdhouse for small birds in the garden helps control insect pests.

If dandelions were hard to grow, they would be most welcome on any lawn.

... Andrew Mason, M.D.

Pecan Tart

for crust:
8 ounces sweet butter, room temperature
1/3 cup sugar
1 teaspoon vanilla
1 large egg
2 1/2 cups flour, unsifted

for filling:
3/4 cup brown sugar
1 teaspoon soft butter
1 teaspoon vanilla
dash of salt
1/2 cup pecans, coarsely chopped
1 egg
1/2 cup whole pecans

for topping:
1 1/2 cups powdered sugar
pinch of salt
1/2 teaspoon lemon juice
1 egg white

In today's households, time is a precious commodity. When you visit your nursery, choose perennials that display these low-maintenance characteristics:
Hardy - can withstand cold without special protection.
High tolerance of pests.
High tolerance of various soil types.
Does not require staking.
Little tendency toward self-sowing.

- Beat together the butter and sugar for crust. Add vanilla and egg.
- Stir in the flour or use a food processor. Chill at least 1 hour.
- With your fingers, spread pastry into an 8 inch tart pan to form a shell. Set aside.
- Preheat oven to 325°.
- Beat together the sugar, butter, vanilla, and salt until just smooth. Add the chopped pecans, then beat in the egg.
- Pour into the shell and top with the whole pecans. Bake for 25 minutes, or until the filling is set. Cool and remove from pan.
- Blend all topping ingredients together until smooth. Drizzle over the cooled tart.

Chocolate Madeleinettes

1/2 cup unsweetened cocoa
3/4 cup all purpose flour
1 teaspoon baking powder
3 large eggs
1/2 cup sugar
1 teaspoon pure vanilla extract
5 ounces sweet butter, melted
3 teaspoons Gran Marnier
2 Tablespoons orange peel, grated

- Preheat oven to 400°. Butter the molds of your madeleinette plaques.
- Sift cocoa, flour, and baking powder together and set aside.
- In a food processor or mixer, combine eggs and sugar. Beat at medium speed for approximately 30 seconds, then switch to high speed and beat until mixture has quadrupled in bulk and is very thick. This will take about 10 minutes.
- Add vanilla, Gran Marnier, grated orange peel, and flour mixture. Fold in with a spatula. Next, fold in the melted butter.
- Spoon a rounded teaspoon of batter into each mold of the plaque. Each mold should be about 3/4 filled. Bake on a lower shelf in the oven for 10 to 12 minutes. Madeleinettes should be softly browned around the edges and bottoms.

More reasons to love chocolate:

- Chocolate is an energy booster. The energy derived from a fat like cocoa butter is 2 1/2 times that of a pure carbohydrate.

- Studies show people, especially women, claim that chocolate boosts their spirits.

- Cocoa is a complex blend of 500 flavor components, so few things come close to matching the flavor.

Toasted Walnut Tart with Wild Blackberry Sauce and Crème Fraîche

Low Maintenance
Flowers:
Daffodil
Goldenrod
Jacob's Ladder
Oriental Poppy
Sunflower
Bluebells
Yucca

for tart shell:
1 1/4 cups flour
1/8 teaspoon salt
2 Tablespoons sugar
1/4 cup sweet butter
1 egg yolk
3 Tablespoons water

for filling:
4 eggs
1 cup heavy cream
1/4 cup clear honey
2 Tablespoons brown sugar
1 1/2 cups toasted walnuts, coarsely chopped
crème fraîche, for topping

for Wild Blackberry Sauce:
2 cups fresh wild blackberries
1/4 cup sugar, to taste
juice of 1 fresh lemon

- Preheat oven to 400°.
- Mix the egg yolk for the shell with the water. Blend well. Set aside.
- Place the remaining shell ingredients into a large bowl and work with your hands until you have a lumpy yellow mixture. Add the yolk and water mixture and mix rapidly with your fingers until all the ingredients are well blended and cohere into a ball. Take care not to overmix.
- Roll the dough on a lightly floured board to about 1/4 inch thickness. Place a 9 or 10 inch flan ring about 1 inch high onto a cookie sheet. Roll the pastry dough onto the rolling

pin and transfer it onto the flan ring. Ease the pastry down inside the ring, taking care not to break it. Press along the sides and bottom. With a knife, cut off the excess dough, following along the contour of the ring.

- Line the dough with waxed paper and fill it up with rice or dried beans to weigh it down.
- Bake for 20 minutes. Remove the waxed paper and filler. Place the shell back in the oven for another 8 to 10 minutes, until the inside is slightly browned. Remove from the oven and let cool at room temperature.
- Preheat oven to 425°.
- In a bowl, beat together all filling ingredients except walnuts. Use a wire whisk, being careful not to overwork.
- Add walnuts, tossing until nuts are coated.
- Distribute the filling evenly inside the tart shell. Bake for 15 to 20 minutes.
- Put all the sauce ingredients into a food processor and purée until smooth. Strain to remove the seeds and set aside.
- To serve, put blackberry sauce on individual serving plates. Position a slice of tart on plate. Sift powdered sugar heavily over tart. Top with crème fraîche.

Sour cream makes a ready substitute when crème fraîche is unavailable.

Apple Blueberry Cream Puff with Champagne Sabayon

for puff pastry:
1/4 cup water
1/4 cup whole milk
2 eggs
4 Tablespoons sweet butter
1/2 cup unbleached or all-purpose flour
1/2 teaspoon sugar
1/4 teaspoon salt

Usually, sweet wines are served with dessert. Sherry, port, angelica, and muscatel are commonly offered after the meal. We, however, still find champagne hard to beat at any time, including with dessert.

for filling:
3 apples, peeled, cored, and sliced lengthwise
2 Tablespoons butter
2 Tablespoons granulated sugar
1 Tablespoon Gran Marnier, additional to taste
1 Tablespoon Cognac, additional to taste
1 teaspoon freshly squeezed lemon juice
1 teaspoon lemon zest
1/2 cup fresh blueberries
1 cup whipped cream
powdered sugar

for sabayon:
1/2 cup sugar
6 egg yolks
1 cup dry champagne

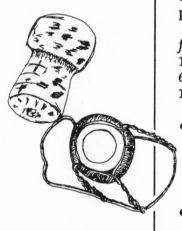

- In a saucepan over low heat, slowly bring to boil the water, butter, sugar, and salt for the puff pastry. Once a boil is achieved, immediately remove saucepan from heat and add milk, then the flour all at once.
- Stir vigorously over medium heat until mixture knits together into a ball, about 30 seconds to 1 minute. Remove the mixture from the heat and cool for a few minutes.
- Add the eggs individually, beating in the first egg thoroughly before adding the next. The

mixture should take on a glossy and smooth appearance, yet be stiff enough to hold its shape when dropped onto a baking sheet. If the mixture is dull, pasty and overly stiff, add more eggs until the consistency is correct.

- Preheat oven to 425°. Line a baking sheet with parchment paper and drop mounds of pastry batter onto the paper a few inches apart, in mounds about 3 inches across.
- Brush each mound of batter with egg wash and bake at 425° for 15 minutes. Then reduce baking temperature to 400° and bake for another 15 minutes.
- Turn off the oven and make a couple of small slits in the side of each puff to vent steam. Prop the oven door open slightly and leave the puffs in the cooling oven for 10 minutes.
- Remove the puffs and cool on wire racks.
- In a sauté pan, melt the butter for the filling with granulated sugar. Add apples, lemon juice, lemon zest, Cognac, and Gran Marnier. Sauté mixture until apples are well coated and take on a warm brown colored. Remove from heat and gently toss in the blueberries.
- Place sabayon ingredients in a saucepan and bring to a lukewarm temperature. Whip together over very low heat for about 10 minutes. Do not allow the mixture to become too hot, you should be able to put your finger into the mixture without discomfort.
- To serve, place lukewarm sabayon on the bottom of warmed plates. Cut the puff pastries in half and place the bottom half of a puff pastry onto each plate. Top with a dollop of whipped cream, the apple/blueberry sauté and cover with the top half of pastry. Sift heavily with powdered sugar. More sabayon may be added, if desired. Add a garnish of your choice.

We don't know who we are until we see what we can do.
... Martha Grimes

Chocolate Mint Roulade with Fresh Raspberry Sauce

According to the diaries of English Jesuit Thomas Gage, in 1698, the women of Chiapa Real, Mexico, had murdered a certain bishop who forbade them to drink chocolate during the mass. Rumor had it, the bishop was poisoned by a cup of tainted chocolate.

for Chocolate Mint Roulade:
3 Tablespoons cocoa powder
1/2 cup flour, sifted
1/4 teaspoon cream of tartar
1 1/2 teaspoons real vanilla extract
pinch of salt
2/3 cup sugar
4 eggs, separated
powdered sugar

for mint cream filling:
1 cup heavy cream
2 teaspoons real mint extract
2 Tablespoons white Cream de Menthe, more to taste
fresh mint leaves, for garnish

for Fresh Raspberry Sauce:
3 1/2 cups fresh raspberries, reserve a few for garnish
1/4 cup sugar, more to taste
2 Tablespoons fresh squeezed lemon juice

- Lightly grease and flour an 11 inch X 15 Inch jelly roll pan. Line the bottom with parchment paper. Preheat oven to 350°.
- Beat egg yolks in a large bowl until they are well broken up. Add 1/3 cup sugar and continue to beat until mixture is very well blended. Beat in vanilla.
- In a separate copper or stainless steel bowl, beat egg whites until just foamy. Add salt and cream of tartar and continue beating. When mixture holds soft peaks, add remaining sugar and beat until peaks are stiff and shiny.
- Fold flour into the yolk mixture gradually, then slowly add egg white mixture,

combining very gently yet thoroughly.

- Fill the prepared jelly roll pan with batter and bake cake in preheated oven until it springs back when pressed gently with a finger, about 15 minutes.
- Cool cake in pan for a few minutes, then turn it out onto a towel covered with a sheet of parchment paper dusted with cocoa powder.
- Remove parchment paper from the bottom of the cake and trim off any crusts which may have formed during baking. Very carefully roll up the cake with the new parchment paper and secure with a towel. Let cool on the rack.
- Whip all mint filling ingredients until they hold stiff peaks. Set aside in a cool place.
- In a food processor, purée all raspberry sauce ingredients until well blended. Strain through a fine mesh and set aside.
- When cake is cool, gently unroll. Spread cream over the entire cake and roll it up, omitting the paper, of course. You will have excess cream filling, reserve it.
- Sift a heavy layer of powdered sugar over the entire roulade.
- To serve, put down a layer of raspberry sauce on a plate and add a slice, approximately 1 inch, of roulade, standing vertically. Sift powdered sugar over the roulade and plate. Add a dollop of the reserved mint cream along the side of the roulade. Garnish with fresh chopped mints and fresh raspberries.

Wine glasses should only be filled halfway. The bouquet, or aroma, of the wine adds greatly to its taste. The best shaped glasses, those with wide mouths, enhance the bouquet of the wine.

Strawberry Meringue Torte with Fresh Apricot Sauce

for Fresh Apricot Sauce:
1 pound fresh apricots
1 Tablespoon fresh squeezed lemon juice
1 to 3 Tablespoons sugar, to taste
3 Tablespoons apricot brandy

List of French recipes from a 1944 cookbook:
- Creole Crab
- Fish Fritters
- Pork Liverloaf
- Corn/Sausage
    Casserole
- Beef Hash Normandie
- Asparagus with
    Cheese
- Potato Patties
- Eggplant Oriental
- Cheese Toast

for Strawberry Meringue Torte:
3/4 cup sugar
6 egg whites
1 1/2 Tablespoons cornstarch
1 cup toasted almonds
butter
flour

for strawberry and whipped cream fillings:
1 basket fresh strawberries, cleaned and sliced
1 Tablespoon sugar
1 squeeze of fresh lemon juice
1 cup heavy cream, with a dash of sugar

- Par boil apricots briefly, 30 seconds to 1 minute. Drop into cold water, remove skins and pits. (If fresh apricots are unavailable, substitute canned apricots, 1 can, drained, and omit sugar.)
- In a food processor, blend apricots with sugar, lemon juice, and brandy until the appropriate consistency is achieved. Set aside
- Butter and flour a cookie sheet and 2 tart rings, 9 inch in diameter, 1 inch in height. Position rings on cookie sheet. Preheat oven to 350°.
- In a food processor, grind almonds to a fine powder and then blend in 1/4 cup sugar. In a separate bowl, mix the remaining 1/2 cup of

sugar with the cornstarch and add in the almonds. Blend well.

- Whip the egg whites until they hold a nice peak and quickly fold them into the almond/sugar mixture.
- Pour the batter into the prepared tart rings and bake for 20 to 25 minutes. Cool on racks.
- Toss strawberries in lemon juice and sugar until they are well coated. Whip cream, with a dash of sugar, to a soft peak.
- Spread whipped cream on first layer of the cake. Arrange strawberries on top of whipped cream. Flip next layer of cake on top of strawberries, with bottom facing up, and cover entire torte with remaining whipped cream. Arrange remaining strawberries on top of torte and cover sides with coarsely ground toasted almonds. Sift a heavy layer of powdered sugar over entire torte.
- Place Fresh Apricot Sauce on a plate and then add a slice of torte. Add more sauce, if desired, and garnish with fresh strawberries, apricots or even a chocolate sauce.

Tips from a 1904 cookbook:

- Gruels are more tempting to the sick if whipped to a froth with an egg-beater before serving in a pretty cup.

- Prune pies are improved by adding 1 teaspoon of vinegar to each pie.

- Corn meal mush will brown very quickly when fried, if a little sugar is put in the water while boiling.

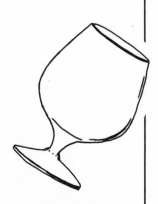

To prevent the juice of pies from soaking into the crust, beat an egg well, and with a bit of cloth dipped into the egg, rub it over the crust before adding the filling.

Raspberry Mousse in Brandy Snap Baskets with Orange and Raspberry Creams

for Brandy Snap Baskets:
1/3 cup light brown sugar, packed firmly
1 1/2 teaspoon ground ginger
3 Tablespoons brandy
3 Tablespoons light corn syrup
3/4 cup flour
1/3 cup butter, in chunks
orange slices and edible flowers, for garnish

for Raspberry Mousse:
2 cups fresh raspberries, washed and dried
1 envelope unflavored gelatin
1/2 cup superfine sugar
1/4 cup fresh squeezed lemon juice
2 whole eggs
2 egg yolks
1 cup heavy cream

for orange cream:
4 Tablespoons orange juice concentrate, at room temperature
1/2 cup heavy cream

for raspberry cream:
4 Tablespoons raspberries, puréed and strained
1 teaspoon sugar
1 teaspoon fresh squeezed lemon juice
1/2 cup heavy cream

- Preheat oven to 350°. Grease a baking sheet.
- In a small saucepan over low heat, cook the butter, corn syrup, and brown sugar, stirring occasionally until butter liquefies. Mix in ginger and brandy and remove from heat.
- Sift the flour into a bowl and stir in the liquid until all ingredients are well mixed.

- Drop teaspoonfuls of batter a few inches apart onto the well-greased baking sheet. Bake in the oven for about 6 minutes, or until brandy snaps are golden brown.
- Remove the cookies one at a time from the baking sheet and mold into baskets over a small inverted measuring cup, or anything you can find which provides the appropriate shape. Set aside to cool.
- In a food processor, purée the raspberries for the mousse. Strain purée to remove the seeds and set aside.
- In a large bowl, whip eggs, yolks, and sugar until mixture thickens considerably.
- In a small saucepan, dissolve gelatin in lemon juice over low heat. Once gelatin is thoroughly dissolved, pour contents of the saucepan very slowly into the egg/sugar mixture and whip until well combined.
- Add the raspberry purée and mix well.
- In a separate bowl, whip cream to soft peaks and set aside.
- With a bowl over ice, stir mousse until it achieves soft peaks. Remove from ice and fold in whipped cream. Immediately pour mousse into Brandy Snap Baskets and refrigerate until mousse sets, approximately 2 1/2 hours.
- Very slowly mix juice concentrate and cream. Whip gently until sauce thickens slightly.
- Mix raspberries puréed for raspberry cream with the sugar and lemon. Slowly mix in the cream. Whip gently until the sauce thickens.
- To serve, cover half an individual serving plate with orange sauce and the other half with the raspberry sauce. Place a Brandy Snap Basket filled with mousse in the center of the plate and sift powdered sugar heavily over the entire plate. Garnish with fresh raspberries, slices of orange, and flowers.

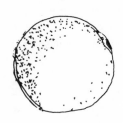

A good meal ought to begin with hunger.
... **French Proverb**

Orange-Chive Sorbet

2/3 cup granulated sugar
2 cups cold water
2 cups fresh squeezed orange juice
1/4 cup fresh chives, chopped
lemon juice, to taste

- Place sugar and water into a saucepan and boil until the sugar dissolves, about 3 minutes. Cool syrup to room temperature.
- Squeeze the orange juice into a bowl. Add th sugar syrup slowly to the juice, stirring until very well mixed. Taste this mixture for appropriate sweetness. If too sweet, add lemon juice to taste.
- Add chives to the mixture and stir well.
- Pour mixture into an ice cream canister and freeze in the ice cream maker according to manufacturer's specifications until sorbet holds its shape.
- To serve, garnish completed sorbet with fres chive sprigs and fresh chive blossoms.

If you do not have an ice cream freezer, you can make sorbet with a food processor. Freeze the mixture, taking care not to let it get too hard, then break it up in a food processor and refreeze. Repeat this process a couple of times until the consistency is smooth.

Sugar Syrup:

2 cups water
1 cup sugar

Combine the water and the sugar in a saucepan. Simmer, stirring occassionally, until the sugar dissolves. Cool, and refrigerate in a closed jar. Use as needed.
Yield 3 cups.

Honeydew-Lime Sorbet

1 medium size ripe honeydew melon
1/2 cup sugar syrup
1/2 to 3/4 cup fresh squeezed lime juice, to taste

- Remove seeds from melon and extract fruit from the rind. Cut melon into 1 inch cubes.
- In a food processor, process melon, sugar syrup, and lime juice into a smooth purée. Pour mixture into an ice cream canister and freeze in the ice cream maker according to manufacturer's specifications until sorbet holds its shape.

Minted Grapefruit Sorbet

2 cups fresh squeezed grapefruit juice
1/2 cup sugar, or to taste
1/4 cup chardonnay
1/2 cup fresh mint, finely chopped
1 teaspoon real mint extract
whole mint leaves, for garnish

- In a saucepan, blend grapefruit juice, sugar, chardonnay, fresh mint, and mint extract. Gently warm until sugar dissolves.
- Pour mixture into an ice cream canister. Freeze in the ice cream maker according to manufacturer's specifications until sorbet holds its shape. Garnish with mint leaves.

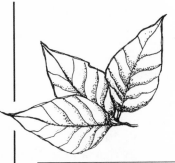

Nothing beats a dry wine or citrus sorbet as a palate cleanser.

- Mark

Merlot Sorbet

1 1/2 cup fresh lemon juice
2 cups water
1/2 cup sugar, more to taste
1 cup Merlot wine

- Mix lemon juice, water, sugar, and Merlot in a saucepan. Gently warm until sugar is dissolved. Cool.
- Pour mixture into an ice cream canister and freeze in the ice cream maker according to manufacturer's specifications until sorbet holds its shape.

It is not the years in your life, but the life in your years that counts!

... Adlai Stevenson

Pinot Noir Oregano Sorbet

An Italian, Carlo Gatti, first introduced ice cream to the general public in 1860. His recipe used a custard base, very similar to present-day French vanilla ice cream. The commercial ice cream we know today became available a little more than a half century ago.

---

1 1/2 cup fresh lemon juice
2 cups water
1/2 cup sugar
1 cup pinot noir wine
1/3 cup fresh oregano, finely chopped

- Mix lemon juice, water, sugar, and wine in a saucepan. Gently warm mixture until the sugar is dissolved.
- Add oregano to the mixture. Cool and pour into an ice cream canister. Freeze in the ice cream maker according to manufacturer's specifications until sorbet holds its shape.

Champagne Sorbet

Brut means the driest Champagne; *extra sec* means less dry; *sec*, dry; *demi-sec*, sweet; *doux*, very sweet. *Demi-sec* and *doux* Champagnes are good with dessert.

Champagne *Blanc de Blancs* means one made entirely from white grapes, whereas most Champagne is made from a mixture of red and white grapes. All Champagnes are blends, but vintage Champagnes are blends of wines of a single year.

---

1 1/2 cup fresh lemon juice
2 cups water
1/2 cup sugar
1 1/4 cups good champagne

- Mix lemon juice, water, sugar, and champagne in a saucepan. Gently warm mixture until the sugar is dissolved.
- Cool and pour into an ice cream canister. Freeze in the ice cream maker according to manufacturer's specifications until sorbet holds its shape.

Carter Facts

The Carter House Inn is a bed and breakfast located in Humboldt County, the heart of the Redwood Empire. An eclectic mix of people, history, culture, and natural wonders makes the county an interesting place to visit. Carter House is on 3rd Street in Eureka, just off Highway 101 and at the gateway of historic Old Town and the waterfront. There are many ways to get there including by car, airplane, and boat.

Rates at the Carter House vary. Four of the rooms have private baths and a suite is available, complete with fireplace, jacuzzi, and an adjoining additional guest room. The decor of the inn is beautifully understated with well-chosen, well-placed antiques, and contemporary ceramics and paintings by local artists. A sumptuous, multi-course breakfast is included in the price of the room. Many of Eureka's most interesting sights are within walking distance.

Across the street from Carter House is Hotel Carter. An intimate twenty rooms, the hotel is known for the same graciousness, warmth, and quality that made Carter House famous. In each room, guests find modern bathrooms (some with jacuzzis), original local art, and fine flowers. Televisions are tucked away inside antique amoires, and the beds, all queen-size, are fitted with down comforters. The price of the room includes a continental breakfast of homemade pastries, fruits, juices, and regional delicacies. Complimentary afternoon wine and hors d'oeuvres are served in the hotel lobby. The hotel's dining room serves world class dinners at very reasonable prices.

An afternoon's drive from San Francisco, both the inn and the hotel are always in demand, so reservations should be made well in advance. Corporate and Frequent Visitor rates are available upon request. For reservations or more information, call (707) 444-8062 or (707) 445-1390, or write to:

Carter House Inn
1033 3rd Street
Eureka, Ca 95501

Hotel Carter
301 L Street
Eureka, Ca 95501

Index

Meats
  Apple / Sausage Sauté in Phyllo 80
  Filet Mignon 98
  Lamb with Honey / Mustard Sauce 99
  Lamb with Stuffed Nasturtiums 100
  Meats and Cheeses 48
  Rabbit with Basil Cream Sauce 96
Menus 112
Merlot Sorbet 143
Mexican Toasted Almond Cookies 128
Minted Grapefruit Sorbet 143
Morning Glory Muffins 29
Morning Potatoes 46
Orange Tea Muffins 33
Orange-Chive Sorbet 142
Pancetta 48
Pastries
  Almond Phyllo Tart 119
  Almond Torte with Raspberries 120
  Apple / Sausage Sauté in Phyllo 80
  Apple Almond Tart 122
  Apple Blueberry Cream Puff 134
  Hazelnut-Mocha Torte 126
  Kiwi Puff Pastry 128
  Pecan Tart 130
  Poached Egg in Puff Pastry 40
  Puff Pastry Dough 117
  Shrimp Spinach Cheese Turnovers 44
  Strawberry Meringue Torte 138
  Vegetable Omelet in Puff Pastry 43
  Walnut Tart 132
Pea Soup with Mint Crème Fraîche 74
Pears in Zinfandel Sauce 25
Pecan Tart 130
Peppermint 52
Peppers 69
Pinot Noir Oregano Sorbet 144
Poached Egg in Puff Pastry 40
Poached Eggs with Asiago Cheese Sauce 37

Prosciutto 48
Puff Pastry Dough 117
Pumpkin Soup 67
Purée of Fennel and Broccoli 106
Quail with Grilled Pears 103
Quinoa 107
Rabbit with Basil Cream Sauce 96
Rainbow Trout 95
Raspberry 52
Raspberry Mousse in Baskets 140
River Trout and Pancetta 82
Roquefort 48
Salmon Cakes 90
Salmon with Tri-Colored Salsa 92
Salsa 92
Sauces
  Apricot Sauce 138
  Asiago Cheese Sauce 37, 42
  Basil Cream Sauce 96
  Beurre Blanc Sauce 89
  Brown Garlic Sauce 80
  Champagne Sabayon 134
  Cilantro Cream Sauce 82
  Cognac Cream Sauce 98
  Cognac Saffron Cream 64
  Creme Anglaise 124
  Dijon-Hollandaise Sauce 34
  Fresh Sage Sauce 102
  Gran Marnier Creme Anglaise 12
  Hollandaise 43
  Honey / Mustard Sauce 99
  Lemon Cream Sauce 61, 82
  Mango / Cilantro / Lime Sauce 88
  Mustard Wine Sauce 62
  Orange Champagne Sauce 34
  Orange Cream 140
  Orange Rosemary Sauce 59
  Raspberry / Mustard Glaze 100
  Raspberry Cream 140

Travel Notes

More Great Flavors from the Pacific Northwest

Cafe Beaujolais
by Margaret S. Fox and John Bear
Recipes and stories from an extraordinary little restaurant in Mendocino, California. As the venerable New York Times put it: "Redwood forests are nearby and the Pacific Ocean is a mile away. The scent of salt air mingles with the smell of something good baking in the Fox kitchen...[Margaret Fox's] hearty breakfasts, earthy black bean chili, ample hamburgers, and richly creative desserts have won her accolades from food and wine publications and food critics ...
Paperback, 224 pages

Morning Food
by Margaret S. Fox and John Bear
"*Morning Food* shares the soul-warming charms of the cuisine of the Cafe Beaujolais—from brawn-building breakfast burritos filled with scrambled eggs, and a streusel-caramel cake, to a crunchy noodle frittata." —*Elle* magazine
Paperback, 208 pages

The Streamliner Diner Cookbook
by Irene Clark, Liz Matteson, Alexandra Rust, and Judith Weinstock
Recipes from the popular Puget Sound hideaway restaurant, featuring diner food like you've never had it before. This is down home gone downtown, with such treats as Dad's Chicken Pot Pie, Hunter's Stew over Polenta, and the baked goods that make locals say "nothing could be finer than breakfast at the diner."
Paperback, 192 pages

The Seattle Classic Cookbook
by the Seattle Junior League
A collection of more than 500 recipes from the Seattle Junior League defines the Pacific Northwestern regional cuisine, focusing on the abundance of natural ingredients, particularly fresh fruits, vegetables, and glorious seafood, and the cooking techniques brought by European and Asian settlers.
Paperback, 320 pages

For more information, or to order, call the publisher at the number below. We accept VISA, Mastercard, and American Express. You may also wish to write for our free catalog of over 500 books, posters, and audiotapes.

TEN SPEED PRESS
P.O. Box 7123
Berkeley, CA 94707
800-841-BOOK